*of Modern Fiction*

ESSAYS IN
PRACTICAL CRITICISM

# The Technique
# of Modern Fiction

ESSAYS IN
PRACTICAL CRITICISM

by Jonathan Raban

Edward Arnold

© Jonathan Raban 1968

*First published 1968 by*
Edward Arnold (Publishers) Ltd.

25 Hill Street, London W1X 8LL

*Reprinted 1972*

Paper edition ISBN: 0 7131 5397 0

*Reprinted 1976*

*Printed offset in Great Britain by*
*Unwin Brothers Limited, The Gresham Press, Old Woking, Surrey*

# Contents

# Acknowledgements

The author and publisher wish to acknowledge the kind permission given by Martin Secker & Warburg Limited to reprint extracts from *Anglo-Saxon Attitudes* by Angus Wilson, *The End of the Road* by John Barth, *The Children of Sánchez* by Oscar Lewis, *The Sot-Weed Factor* by John Barth, and 'Sermon' by James Purdy; by Hutchinson and Co. (Publishers) Ltd. to reprint an extract from *The Pumpkin Eater* by Penelope Mortimer; by Longmans, Green & Co. Ltd. to reprint an extract from *Flight into Camden* by David Storey; by Chatto and Windus Ltd. to reprint extracts from *The Sandcastle* by Iris Murdoch, and *The Hamlet* by William Faulkner; by George Weidenfeld & Nicolson Ltd. to reprint extracts from *Jerusalem the Golden* by Margaret Drabble, *Herzog* by Saul Bellow, *The Group* by Mary McCarthy, and *Pale Fire* by Vladimir Nabokov; by André Deutsch Ltd. to reprint extracts from *Goodbye Columbus* by Philip Roth, and *The Emperor of Ice Cream* by Brian Moore; by Miss Sonia Brownell and Martin Secker and Warburg Ltd. to reprint an extract from *Nineteen Eighty-Four* by George Orwell; by Eyre and Spottiswoode (Publishers) Ltd. to reprint an extract from *The Magic Barrel* by Bernard Malamud; by Methuen & Co. Ltd. to reprint an extract from *A Single Man* by Christopher Isherwood; by the Executors of the Ernest Hemingway Estate and Jonathan Cape Ltd. to reprint extracts from *The First Forty-Nine Stories*; by Macmillan & Co. Ltd. to reprint an extract from *The Problem of Knowledge* by A. J. Ayer; by the Trustees of the Hardy Estate and Macmillan & Co. Ltd. to reprint an extract from *The Woodlanders* by Thomas Hardy; by The Bodley Head to reprint an extract from *Ulysses*, by James Joyce; by T. Werner Laurie to reprint an extract from *Oil!* by Upton Sinclair; by Hamish Hamilton Ltd. to reprint an extract from *La Nausée* by Jean-Paul Sartre; by A. D. Peters & Co. to reprint an extract from *Love among the Ruins* by Evelyn Waugh; by Le Carré Productions Ltd. and Victor Gollancz Ltd. to reprint an extract from *The Spy who came in from the Cold* by John Le Carré; by Michael Joseph Ltd. to reprint an extract from *Billy Liar* by Keith Waterhouse; by MacGibbon & Kee Ltd. to reprint an extract from *Talking to Women* by Nell Dunn; by Penguin Books Ltd. to reprint an extract from *The Day of the Locust* by Nathanael West; by Laurence Kitchin to reprint an extract from 'The Decline of the Western'; by the Clarendon Press, Oxford, to reprint an extract from *Fowler's Modern English Usage* revised by Sir Ernest Gowers; by William Heinemann Ltd., Laurence Pollinger Ltd. and the Estate of the Late Mrs. Frieda Lawrence to reprint an extract from *Women in Love* by D. H. Lawrence; and by Random House Inc. to reprint an extract from *Invisible Man* by Ralph Ellison.

# Introduction

## 1. The Novel and the 1960s

Three recent publications highlight a central issue of most general discussions of modern fiction. In 1961 Oscar Lewis, an American anthropologist, published *The Children of Sánchez*, an edited series of tape recordings in which a family from Mexico City talk about themselves. Lewis changed the name of the family and translated the conversations from Spanish into English, obliterating his own questions and contributions. In addition, he arranged his material so that it acquired structural unity and narrative coherence. *The Children of Sánchez* reads 'like a novel' in that it recreates the world it describes, using all the resources of the technique of fiction. In 1966 a novelist, Truman Capote, repaid the compliment with the publication of a 'non-fiction novel', *In Cold Blood*. Capote's book anatomized a real murder, but invented conversations and entered into the minds of the participants with a fiction-writer's licence. In 1967, William Manchester, author of a documentary history of the Dallas weekend, answered questions on British television about his book *Death of a President*. When asked why the account was so 'excessively' detailed he replied that he had wanted to give his work 'the veracity of fiction'.

It seems that recently the art of fiction and the skills of history and sociology have impinged so closely on one another that in some cases they are inextricably entwined. The facts offer a variety of interpretations. At the facile end of the scale lies the assertion that the social sciences have 'killed off' the novel. Or, if one prefers to go to the other extreme, one can argue that sociology and anthropology have 'freed' the novel from social representation just as the camera 'freed' painting from illustration. The novel, say these observers, can now move on to allegory, romance and symbol, bereft of its traditional social connotations. Neither of these speculations appears to make much sense when we test it against the actual body of fiction now being written in this country and the United States. Possibly the novelists have yet to catch up with the theorists; more likely, simplistic theories of this kind are well off the target.

One might best approach the question from the point of view of the social scientists: what have they discovered in the novel that their own disciplines do not possess? Manchester found a special 'veracity'; Oscar Lewis found a technique of control and selection. In other words they took as the essential constituent of the novel, not a subject matter, but a form and a method. Lewis is indebted to the tradition of the American novel in *The Children of Sánchez*. Interestingly, the writers from whom he has learned most are not the social realists like Theodore Dreiser or Frank Norris who also wrote of the lives of the urban poor. Instead Lewis has gone to the masters of selection and point of view. Mark Twain's management of vernacular narrative and Henry James's doctrine of 'continuous relevance' are among the antecedents of Lewis's beautifully structured account.

In her study of Sartre, Iris Murdoch has talked of the novelist's 'blessed freedom from rationalism'. The special attribute of the novel is that it offers a form which can order experience without imposing a *logical* consistency on the elements of that experience. What has been discovered in the novel is its essential *contingency*, its capacity to include things on a criterion of aesthetic rather than causal relevance. *Death of a President* is packed with incidental detail, observations which belong to a total impression of the events, but which cannot be explained in terms of any logical relationship to the Kennedy assassination. Manchester saw these details as inherent features of the novel, part of the fabric of the peculiar 'truth' of fiction.

Oscar Lewis broadens the picture in his introduction to *The Children of Sánchez*:

> In this volume I offer the reader a deeper look into the lives of one of these families by the use of a new technique whereby each member of the family tells his own life-story in his own words. This approach gives us a cumulative, multi-faceted, panoramic view of each individual, of the family as a whole, and of many aspects of lower-class Mexican life. The independent versions of the same incidents given by the various family members provide a built-in check upon the reliability and validity of much of the data and thereby partially offset the subjectivity inherent in a single auto-biography. At the same time it reveals the discrepancies in the way events are recalled by each member of the family.

Conventional methods of anthropology concentrate on analysis and explanation of the given data. Lewis chose to adopt a technique of selective revelation, allowing the reader to draw his own conclusions from the 'cumulative, multi-faceted, panoramic view of each individual'. Discrepancies in the various accounts are left without interpretative comment: if we follow the narratives sufficiently carefully we shall notice them for ourselves. 'Dramatize! Dramatize!' said Henry James. Lewis has dramatized his material superbly. The rationalist equipment of anthropology has been stripped away, leaving the reverberant texture of Sánchez family life to speak for itself. This is not to suggest that Lewis has not ordered the experience he presents, but he has ordered it 'novelistically' rather than 'scientifically'. He sketches, though understates, his real achievement when he writes:

> I hope that this method preserves for the reader the emotional satisfaction and understanding which the anthro-pologist experiences in working directly with his subjects but

which is only rarely conveyed in the formal jargon of anthropological monographs.

This kind of cross-fertilization between the novel and other disciplines has been particularly useful in that it has helped to redefine the novelist's proper territory. On occasions, notably during the nineteen-thirties with the rise and fall of the 'proletarian novel', writers of fiction have seemed to be unhappy trespassers on other men's ground. Certainly there have been plenty of twentieth-century novels which are no more than thinly fictionalized political commentaries or sociological case-histories. More recently, I think that there has been a growing awareness of the novel's real possibilities as a form, and a new confidence in the idea that the descriptive techniques of the novelist give him a unique advantage over the rational analyst. The examples in this book testify to a reawakened interest in the form and structure of the novel. Several of them also reveal a fascination with the capacity of the novel to deal with 'contingent' experience. The confrontation between the social sciences and the novel has given a special urgency to the question 'What can the novelist do that no other commentator can?' Some of the possible answers can, I think, be sampled here.

During the course of this book we shall be examining some of the technical qualities of the new media which have been absorbed by the novel. The tape recorder has made us listen to the way that people speak with a new sensitivity; both dialogue and narrative have been stimulated to a greater accuracy in echoing the exact tones of the spoken word. Similarly, the visual techniques of the film and television director have sometimes been translated into literary terms with considerable success.

Television has wrought more general changes on the texture of the novel. Marshall McLuhan has, somewhat pompously, claimed that television is turning the world into a 'global village', condensing boundaries of class and nationality. On a limited scale this is demonstrably true. A characteristic failure of the nineteenth-century English novelist was his inability to transcend his own social group and regional locality. Trollope's appalling cartoons of working-class characters were symptomatic of his period. I doubt that any contemporary novelist could get by on Trollope's scant social equipment: the writer, his characters and his audience know each other more intimately—they share the same programmes, see the same advertisements, react to the same ubiquitous personalities. Television has vastly extended our cultural common ground, and that common ground is the novelist's traditional terrain. 'Stick to Bath,' advised Jane Austen. Today, however, Bath is as culturally close to York or Lancaster as it is to Bristol. Television, together with popular journalism, has universalized manners and fashion. As a result the novelist has an unprecedented range of reference. If the fiction of the present is still read in a hundred years' time it will probably require an even larger body of scholarly apparatus than Pope's *Dunciad* does today. But Pope's audience was based on literary London; it was a comparatively select group of knowledgeable *litterateurs*. Most of the references in the contemporary novel are available to a mass audience, educated into knowingness by the small screen.

Novelists themselves come from a rather wider range of social backgrounds than their predecessors, as Raymond Williams has shown in *The Long Revolution*. His findings can be confirmed by a glance at the bibliography at the end of this book. Of English writers, one attended a secondary modern school; others are fairly equally divided between grammar and public schools. Some attended Oxford or Cambridge universities; some went to provincial universities; some didn't go to university at all. Correspondingly, the novelist's audience is more broadly based as a result of successive education acts and an increasing area of leisure time. In recent years modern fiction has moved into school and college syllabi. Sixth-formers read William Golding for Advanced Level G.C.E.; university students encounter Saul Bellow in courses on Modern American Literature.

This general expansion of readership is linked to the greater availability of modern writing in an inexpensive format, combined with mass distribution backed by a system of large-scale promotion. The 'paperback revolution' of the 1930s and '40s paralleled the rapid growth of cheap book production which attended the development of the railways a century before. Under the direction of Sir Allen Lane, Penguin books, together with John Lehmann's *Penguin New Writing* series, helped to popularize the work of serious contemporary writers. It is now reasonable to expect that any well-reviewed novel will be cheaply available in paperback within two or three years of its first publication.

Recently the state, through the medium of the Arts Council, has taken a hand in the development of contemporary writing. In 1966 bursaries were awarded to a small number of practising authors. When they were announced they sparked off a long-drawn-out public controversy: they were not large enough; they had been given to the wrong people; they were too large and there were not enough of them, and so on. The dispute, maintained in the correspondence columns and editorials of the *Times Literary Supplement*, tended to obscure the one really important fact: that the state now considered that fiction-writing was an occupation worthy of organized assistance. In 1967, budgetary concessions on tax payable on authors' royalties may be seen to have underlined the point.

## 2. *Practical Criticism and the Novel*

Obviously the primary subject of this book is the variety and flexibility of recent novels and short stories. But at the same time the book tries to suggest a critical approach to the technique of fiction. There is already in existence an influential body of Practical Criticism. C. B. Cox and A. E. Dyson have sketched the origins, history and practice of the technique in their books *The Practical Criticism of Poetry* and *Modern Poetry*. Under their editorship *The Critical Quarterly* has provided us with exemplary critiques of individual works. In its application as an academic discipline, Practical Criticism has encouraged a large number of students to discover the technical intricacies of both poetry and fiction.

But to use a scheme of close verbal analysis at all is to commit oneself to a process of selection and exclusion: many passages, of both prose and poetry, simply defy analysis when they are removed from their contexts. One must be careful to avoid turning this selection into a form of value judgement. Because piece (*a*) works in a compressed space and invites detailed analysis, it is in no way necessarily 'better' than piece (*b*) which functions adequately only in the larger context of the whole novel or poem. This difficulty arises far more frequently when one is selecting passages of prose than when one is dealing with poetry. While I was compiling a list of extracts to include in this book, I had to reject many of my original proposals. Although the complete novels illustrated very well the kind of point I was trying to make, no one-thousand-word extract from them demonstrated the issue sufficiently tellingly. Consequently there was a real danger of setting up two quite distinct categories of modern fiction: the kind, illustrated here, which works in detail over a short space, and the kind, excluded from specific discussion in this book, which gains its effects cumulatively over many pages. The existence of this problem should act as a warning to the critic: when we apply the techniques of Practical Criticism to a novel we should realize that they have only a limited value. They belong to descriptive rather than evaluative criticism in any case. Provided that the piece under discussion is itself densely worked and makes some kind of sense out of context, then Practical Criticism will probably illuminate it.

But one should not, I think, take the matter further than that.

There is too an essential difference between the quality of attention demanded by a lyric poem and that demanded by a novel. The approach of Practical Criticism to poetry implicitly suggests that all elements of the poem in question can be contained in the mind simultaneously. Only then can the various parts be seen to interact. A poem divides naturally into the brief units of line, image and stanza, and the Practical Critics concentrate almost exclusively on these. Problems of the time lapse between beginning and ending a reading of the poem, and of a narrative sequence which tends to dismiss each event as it deals with it, are rarely involved unless the poem is immensely long.

A novel, on the other hand, divides most easily into the longer units of the paragraph, the episode and the chapter. Our interest is generally sustained, not by images and rhythmic repetitions, but by the organization of events in the narrative. The verbal quality of a novel is best described, not in terms of the striking image or occasional distortion of syntax, but by the continuously maintained effect of the overall tone. As a practical problem in criticism, one might try to decide the best method of explicating the following short passage from William Faulkner's novel *The Hamlet*:

He scrambled up and ran. The cow was quite near and he saw the fire—a tender, rosy, creeping thread low in the smoke between him and the location of the cow's voice. Each time his feet touched the earth now he gave a short shriek like an ejaculation, trying to snatch his foot back before it could have taken his weight, then turning immediately in aghast amazement to the other foot which he had for the moment forgotten, so that presently he was not progressing at all but merely moving in one spot, like a dance, when he heard the horse coming at him again. He screamed. His voice and that of the horse became one voice, wild, furious and without hope, and he ran into and through the fire and burst into air, sun, visibility again, shedding flames which sucked away behind him like a tattered garment.

In the first place the images in this passage ('like a dance', 'like a tattered garment') are surprisingly unstriking. They seem to be used not for emphasis but for punctuation; their use allows a pause between moments of action. Our central interest lies in the narrative flow of the sentences, in the sequence of movements involving cow and boy. Faulkner never allows us to anchor our attention on one object for long. When he gives us a momentary rest, he supplies us with a descriptive simile that is too weak to distract our interest from the main business of the action. Clearly Faulkner's effect works on a much larger scale than that of a lyric poem. Critical emphasis on a single word, image or line would violently distort the rapid and erratic pattern of the prose.

There is another difficulty here. Throughout this chapter of *The Hamlet* Faulkner adopts the point of view of the boy, and his writing follows the sequence of the boy's own thoughts and sensations. We can fully understand any extract from the chapter only if we bring to it all our accumulated knowledge about the boy. We should know, for instance, that he is an idiot; this obviously clarifies the bemused innocence of his violent encounter with the cow.

In prose the study of the language of any one short section is not enough. So much of our appreciation depends on knowledge acquired outside any particular passage—on our judgement of character and our interest in the development of plot and situation. If we are looking for a vocabulary to describe the verbal qualities of fiction, we shall have to find words appropriate to the long, linear units of prose, to the dependence of the language of prose on subject matter and context, and to the generally subservient relationship of language to narrative. In a form which continually invites us to ask 'what happens next?', our attention will be of a very different kind to the uniform concentration which we can exercise on a short poem.

## 3. *The Technique of Modern Fiction*

By modern fiction I mean work published since 1945 by English and American writers who have established their characteristic styles since that date. The definition is one of convenience only. Inevitably many individual careers traverse boundaries of geography and history. Whether one classifies Brian Moore or Christopher Isherwood as an 'English' or as an 'American' author is a matter of personal opinion and I have not attempted to impose distinctions of this kind.

I have arranged the book in three main sections, each consisting of five specific topics. The three sections, on handling the narrative, on dealing with character, and on points of style and language, indicate some of the major critical approaches to fiction. The chapters themselves raise particular issues: how do novelists construct dialogue? how do they select their point of view in the story?—and so on. Each chapter is a 'sandwich', containing an extract from a recent novel or short story surrounded by two slices of critical discussion. In each case I introduce the topic with some general observations, then analyse the extract in the terms set out in the introduction.

The extracts should speak for themselves, and the analyses simply offer close readings of the extracts, but the introductions need some explanation. I have tried wherever possible to tackle each issue on a broad and generalistic front, suggesting some of the ways in which writers of all periods have coped with a particular problem. I have set out to erect a few guidelines for further exploration and to raise critical hares while leaving the reader to track them down. Each aspect of fictional technique is a major research subject, and one cannot hope to do a great deal with it in three or four pages. If the reader can add qualifications and extensions from his own knowledge, this is all to the good. The aim of each introduction is to stimulate enquiry and provoke questions.

This should be a sourcebook from which readers will move out to discover novels and critical ideas for themselves. It is certainly not intended as an authoritative manual. The sample pieces of fiction printed with each chapter are meant as aperitifs, not as digests. Consequently the bibliography at the end is rather more extensive than is usual, for my own brief discussions and illustrations are all pointed in the direction of the list for further reading. Questions of fictional technique can be examined further in detailed articles and books; recent fiction itself is a vast field, of which my reading list shows only a limited sector.

*Narrative*

# 1 Narrative: Some Problems and Conventions

When a story is told, we assume that the action of the story is complete. Narrator and reader recall and reconstruct past events, viewing them with the hindsight of retrospective knowledge. The fairy-tale formula of 'Once upon a time . . . and then they lived happily ever after' neatly encapsulates the action of the story, placing it in a detached perspective: it exists in an ordered sequence, irrelevances eliminated, ready for judgement by the reader. No narrative is, of course, quite as straightforward as that. Anyone who has told a fairytale to a child will know how important it is to phrase dialogue in direct speech, creating the illusion that the conversation is taking place not in the past but in the present. Classical historians made use of the same sort of device when they accentuated the immediacy of climactic events by describing them in the present tense. In order to involve the reader directly in the story, the narrator frequently adopts the convention of pretending that things are happening here and now; imagery and dialogue are made to work before our eyes, as if no gap in time separated us from the action of the narrative. Some elements in the story will be permanent in any case, providing a link between present and past. Towns, buildings and characters may continue to exist long after the action of the story is complete. So Emily Brontë reminds us early in *Wuthering Heights*:

> One step brought us into the family sitting-room, without any introductory lobby or passage: they call it here 'the house' pre-eminently. It includes kitchen and parlour, generally; but I believe at Wuthering Heights the kitchen is forced

to retreat altogether into another quarter: at least I distinguished a chatter of tongues, and a clatter of culinary utensils, deep within.

The existence of the house itself provides the reader with a vital continuity between the various times at which the events of the novel occur. Wuthering Heights is 'still there', bridging our own time with the distant turbulence of Cathy and Heathcliff. Similarly, Scott Fitzgerald informs us at the end of *Tender Is The Night* that Dick Diver his hero is rumoured to be still practising medicine in some small town in New York State. Reader and character are connected by the use of the present tense. If we assume the right of automatic detachment from the events recounted in the narrative, such elements of continuity will tend to blur the distinction. Most narratives mix their tenses: some parts occur in the distant past while some survive into the present, so that the reader is held in a flexible relationship with the events of the story, sometimes involved, sometimes detached. Conventions of tense are, of course, free to be broken, and many novelists have edged their narratives towards one extreme or the other in order to create a special effect. An example of present tense narration will be found in the extract; one might parallel this with the technique used in a novel like *The Sot-Weed Factor* by John Barth where the author forcibly detaches his reader from the story, partly by phrasing it in archaic language, partly by setting it in a 'past-historic' tense.

Choosing the tense of a narrative entails questions of involvement and judgement: how closely does the author wish to let his reader approach the characters and events? That inevitably depends on whoever is telling the story. Sometimes reader and writer collaborate in following the adventures of a third party; sometimes the third party retells his own account in his own words; sometimes the author appears to be writing almost autobiographically, where his 'I' character closely resembles what we know of the author himself. Facile assumptions that a first-person narrative is necessarily more 'intimate' and 'involving' than a third-person narrative are easily disproved. In my own experience I often find it hard to remember whether a particular novel was written in the first or third person, even though I can picture the central character in considerable detail. There are no hard and fast distinctions to be made on matters of person, although some critics have attempted to construct them.[1] What is undeniably important is the occasional aberrant usage of person, where a novelist has drawn special attention to the convention.

We meet this kind of narrative deviancy very forcibly in *Moby Dick*. Melville starts the novel in the first person, telling the story in the words of Ishmael, a wandering sailor. As the book goes on, Ishmael frequently seems to disappear for long periods; often Melville describes events at which Ishmael could not possibly have been present. The ship *The Pequod* is capsized at the end of the novel by Moby Dick, the white whale. All hands—except, miraculously, Ishmael—are lost. Melville's epigraph to *Moby Dick* reads 'I only am escaped alone to tell thee'. Clearly the novel in its present form could hardly exist without the survival of Ishmael to recount the story. Yet Ishmael's escape is implausible; it is an awkward, though necessary, device. Melville needed a living witness, someone who could attest in the first person to the events in the narrative. Ishmael has a similar kind of bridging function to the present-tense elements in narrative I noticed earlier. He links the reader to the characters, providing a degree of rather forced continuity. The value of first-person testimony is obvious, particularly when the events in the story seem so remote or unlikely that the author

[1] A most interesting discussion of the importance of 'person' in fiction by Michel Butor, the modern French novelist, will be found in *New Left Review*, No. 34, November–December 1965. Butor's theory of person is fascinating, but as Wayne Booth has observed in *The Rhetoric of Fiction*, it seems to have little effect on the actual experience of reading a novel.

feels it necessary to construct the figure of a witness who saw everything at first hand. The homely qualities of Ellen Dean who narrates most of *Wuthering Heights* and of the first-person narrator of Edgar Allan Poe's 'The Fall of the House of Usher' act as useful links in the chain between the reader and the bizarre actions of both stories.

Just as on these occasions use of the first person may help to involve the reader more directly in the narrative, so an intermittent use of the third person in a predominantly first-person story can effect a degree of detachment. In *Herzog* Saul Bellow sometimes calls Herzog 'I', sometimes 'he'. These changes do correspond with emotional movements in the narrative. Bellow seems to be trying to emphasize our shifting relationship with his hero, suggesting that we should be detached at one moment and involved the next.

But these self-evidently conscious uses of 'person' as a narrative device are comparatively rare. The majority of first- and third-person narratives do not stand up to a close scrutiny of the author's motive in using a particular pronoun. Frequently they could as well be told with one as with another. Only when the author seems to be deliberately manipulating the conventions should we take critical notice. A good deal of recent fiction, as I think the extract shows, is obviously written with a view to experimenting with the conventions of narrative, exposing the kind of mechanics of story-telling which we would normally take for granted.

## GEORGE

### from *A Single Man* by Christopher Isherwood

*George, a middle-aged Englishman teaching at San Tomas State College, Los Angeles, lives alone in a shambling house on the outskirts of the city. His close friend Jim, with whom he used to share the house, is recently dead. Here, in the first three pages of the novel, George wakes up and prepares himself for the day which forms the subject of the book.*

Waking up begins with saying *am* and *now*. That which has awoken then lies for a while staring up at the ceiling and down into itself until it has recognized *I*, and therefrom deduced *I am, I am now*. *Here* comes next, and is at least negatively reassuring; because *here*, this morning, is where it had expected to find itself; what's called *at home*.

But *now* isn't simply now. *Now* is also a cold reminder; one whole day later than yesterday, one year later than last year. Every *now* is labelled with its date, rendering all past *nows* obsolete, until—later or sooner—perhaps—no, not perhaps— quite certainly: It will come.

Fear tweaks the vagus nerve. A sickish shrinking from what waits, somewhere out there, dead ahead.

But meanwhile the cortex, that grim disciplinarian, has taken its place at the central controls and has been testing them, one after another; the legs stretch, the lower back is arched, the fingers clench and relax. And now, over the entire inter-communication-system, is issued the first general order of the day: UP.

Obediently the body levers itself out of bed—wincing from twinges in the arthritic thumbs and the left knee, mildly nauseated by the pylorus in a state of spasm—and shambles naked into the bathroom, where its bladder is emptied and it is weighed; still a bit over 150 pounds, in spite of all that toiling at the gym! Then to the mirror.

What it sees there isn't so much a face as the expression of a predicament. Here's what it has done to itself, here's the mess it has somehow managed to get itself into, during its fifty-eight years; expressed in terms of a dull harassed stare, a coarsened nose, a mouth dragged down by the corners into a grimace as if at the sourness of its own toxins, cheeks sagging from their anchors of muscle, a throat hanging limp in tiny wrinkled folds. The harassed look is that of a desperately tired swimmer or runner; yet there is no question of stopping. The creature we are watching will struggle on and on until it drops. Not because it is heroic. It can imagine no alternative.

Staring and staring into the mirror, it sees many faces within its face—the face of the child, the boy, the young man, the not-so-young man—all present still, preserved like fossils on superimposed layers, and, like fossils, dead. Their message to this live dying creature is: Look at us—we have died—what is there to be afraid of?

It answers them: But that happened so gradually, so easily. *I'm afraid of being rushed.*

It stares and stares. Its lips part. It starts to breathe through its mouth. Until the cortex orders it impatiently to wash, to shave, to brush its hair. Its nakedness has to be covered. It must be dressed up in clothes because it is going outside, into the world of the other people; and these others must be able to identify it. Its behaviour must be acceptable to them.

Obediently, it washes, shaves, brushes its hair; for it accepts its responsibilities to the others. It is even glad that it has its place among them. It knows what is expected of it.

It knows its name. It is called George.

By the time it has gotten dressed: it has become *he*; has become already more or less George—though still not the whole George they demand and are prepared to recognize. Those who call him on the phone at this hour of the morning would be bewildered, maybe even scared, if they could realize what this three-quarters-human thing is that they are talking to. But, of course, they never could—its voice's mimicry of their George is nearly perfect. Even Charlotte is taken in by it. Only two or three times has she sensed something uncanny, and asked, 'Geo—are you *all right?*'

He crosses the front room, which he calls his study, and comes down the staircase. The stairs turn a corner; they are narrow and steep. You can touch both handrails with your elbows and you have to bend your head—even if, like George, you are only five eight. This is a tightly planned little house. He often feels protected by its smallness; there is hardly room enough here to feel lonely.

Nevertheless—

Think of two people, living together day after day, year after year, in this small space, standing elbow to elbow cooking at the same small stove, squeezing past each other on the narrow stairs, shaving in front of the same small bathroom mirror, constantly jogging, jostling, bumping against each other's bodies by mistake or on purpose, sensually, aggressively, awkwardly, impatiently, in rage or in love—think what deep though invisible tracks they must leave, everywhere, behind them! The doorway into the kitchen has been built too narrow. Two people in a hurry, with plates of food in their hands, are apt to keep colliding here. And it is here, nearly every morning, that George, having reached the bottom of the stairs, has this sensation of suddenly finding himself on an abrupt, brutally broken-off, jagged edge—as though the track had disappeared down a landslide. It is here that he stops short and knows, with a sick newness, almost as though it were for the first time: Jim is dead. Is dead.

He stands quite still, silent, or at most uttering a brief animal grunt, as he waits for the spasm to pass. Then he walks into the kitchen. These morning spasms are too painful to be treated sentimentally. After them, he feels relief, merely. It is like getting over a bad attack of cramp.

ANALYSIS

A crude preliminary classification of the narrative style of *A Single Man* would indicate that it was in 'the third person, present tense'. But this would give no hint of the extraordinary pliancy which Isherwood gives to the form of his story. There are effectively three varieties of tense and four of person, and the shifts from one to another mirror the emotional movements of the narrative.

The dominant transition is one of person. George starts as an 'It', a mere animal object equipped with a biological mechanism. Isherwood (who spent a brief period as a medical student in 1928) records the awakening of this thing in clinical terms. Its feelings are seen as neural phenomena: the vagus nerve, cortex and pylorus twitch into some kind of zoological life.

By the twelfth paragraph when George, washed, shaved and dressed, has become 'three-quarters-human', Isherwood refers to him alternately as both 'It' and 'Him'. But his ambiguous status is resolved in the next paragraph by the intrusion of the second-person pronoun:

> You can touch both handrails with your elbows and you have to bend your head—even if, like George, you are only five eight.

Just as at the beginning we were invited to exercise clinical detachment from George, so now we are asked to identify with him. We and George have our humanness in common. The second-person pronoun is used to forge an intimate link between author, character and reader.

Isherwood continues to address the reader directly in order to bring into existence yet another variety of third person:

> Think of two people, living together day after day, year after year, in this small space, standing elbow to elbow cooking at the same small stove . . .

This device allows George and Jim a momentary existence *in the present*. By persuading the reader to recreate the memory of George's and Jim's life together, Isherwood prepares him for George's renewed awareness of Jim's death and his intense pang of loneliness. 'They' no longer exist; there is only an isolated 'He'.

At first glance, Isherwood's handling of tense may seem more uniform than his handling of person. But although everything appears to be happening in the present there are important distinctions between different kinds of action in the passage. Look, for example, at the first paragraph:

> Waking up begins with saying *am* and *now*. That which has awoken then lies for a while staring up at the ceiling and down into itself until it has recognised *I* . . .

Much of *A Single Man* deals with actions which are habitual and repetitive; George gets up, drives to work, drinks coffee and so on—all things which he was doing long before Jim died. Consequently the ritualized aspects of everyday life afford a way of enabling the past to survive into the present, just as the past still lives in George's face:

> Staring and staring into the mirror, it sees many faces within its face—the face of the child, the boy, the young man, the not-so-young man—all present still, preserved like fossils on superimposed layers, and, like fossils, dead.

Most of the extract is phrased in this 'present-habitual' tense of generalized statement, in which the past is implicated just as deeply as the immediate present. As a result, one of the paradoxical effects of Isherwood's use of the present tense is that it tends to place actions 'beyond time', endowing them with a mythic quality. These, he seems to be saying, are actions common to all times, even, perhaps, to all men. This accounts for the absence of specific detail in many places: Isherwood characteristically indicates that routine actions are taking place, and we can fill in the immediate details for ourselves. In this context it is easy to accept the illusion that Jim is still alive and the house is populated by two people. For in the fifteenth paragraph the present tense is used to convey events which really happened only in the past. Ironically, the rituals have lived on while Jim has died.

The present tense therefore indicates three types of time here: habitual actions which are common to both present and past, immediate actions specifically related to the present moment, and events in the past which give the momentary illusion of continuing into the present. George's own ambivalent preoccupation with the past is charted exactly by the undertones carried by the use of tense in this passage.

There is a very general point worth noticing in connection with the use of present-tense narration. When a story takes place in the past the narrator can call upon his characters to appear when he needs them. Since the narrator knows the outcome of the story he can pick the salient points of its development and show the characters in action at those points only. But in present-tense narrative the narrator must seem to be as unaware as the characters of what will happen next. He cannot compress or select his material; he must ruthlessly follow every action of his central character, leaving nothing out. Consistent use of the present-tense must entail an invasion of the character's privacy. So we follow George even into the lavatory. He is allowed no 'off stage' moments at all.

Such enforced intimacy tends to make the reader identify with George: we tail him so closely that the division between him and ourselves often seems very slender indeed. In this respect *A Single Man* embodies two contradictory forces. On the one hand the tense leads us to involvement with the hero; on the other the use of the third person presents the hero in a detached light. The ambiguous shifts of the extract are characteristic of the whole novel. At the beginning and end of the book we see George as an 'It', while during the action he alternates between being a third-person and being a kind of surrogate first-person standing for Isherwood and the reader. Questions of judgement are consequently very difficult indeed: dare we judge that decaying biological thing when it is we ourselves who may be George?

# 2 Narrative: Point of View

A work of fiction deals by definition with the interaction of characters. In real situations there are obviously as many interpretations of an affair as there are people concerned, since for each person the situation is coloured and defined by his own rôle within it. An outsider is likely to view any conflict through the eyes of the most sympathetic character involved. Watching *Hamlet* for instance, most of us would implicitly adopt Hamlet's own viewpoint. But the play would take on a very different shape if we put ourselves in the place of Polonius or Gertrude. Percy Lubbock, in *The Craft of Fiction*, considered the matter to be pre-eminently important: 'The whole intricate question of method, in the craft of fiction, I take to be governed by the question of the point of view—the question of the relation in which the narrator stands to the story.'

In many stories of course, the narrator stands in a godlike position above his characters, knowing what each of them thinks and feels. But one should be sceptical about accepting the idea of the 'omniscient narrator' too easily. Writers like Henry Fielding and Jane Austen are often credited with 'omniscience' in their narration, yet it is a gift that they exercise sparingly. More often they present the public faces of their characters, much as they might be seen by a detached and sensitive observer. We rarely penetrate to the 'hidden self' of motive and feeling, although we often overhear conversations or catch a character unawares in a way denied to any participant in the story.

A truly omniscient narrator would be a tiresome guide through a novel. He would forever be suppressing his intrusively obvious knowledge of the outcome of the plot and would reveal so much of the characters that they would be so transparent as to be uninteresting. The majority of so-called 'omniscient narrators' are merely efficient spies. In the novels of Fielding and Austen someone has wired the locations with microphones and hidden cameras, while the novelist sits at the control room, monitoring all the information.

> My true name is so well known in the records of registers at Newgate, and in the Old Bailey . . .

begins Daniel Defoe in *Moll Flanders*. Defoe takes up the form of the fictional memoir, becomes completely immersed in his central character and makes us see everything through the eyes of Moll herself. There are clearly severe limitations to this technique: nothing can happen in the novel unless Moll is present or unless someone retails information to her. The author has to make his central character sufficiently engaging to retain our constant interest and must distort all the other characters into the shapes they would naturally assume in the mind of the memoirist. Yet when a novelist sticks to a single point of view, he does achieve a certain fidelity to the conditions of real life. His novel is subject to the same limitations of awareness that are imposed on an actual individual. We as readers are invited to inhabit the body of someone else, to see the world through their eyes, to live in the same partial ignorance and suffer the same narrowing of vision and judgement.

The technique of the single, consistent point of view is open to considerable variation. The narrator may be a character who stands on the fringe of the events in the novel. His main function is to observe, and when he takes a hand in the plot, his rôle is a minor one. Marlow in Joseph Conrad's *Heart of Darkness* and Nick Carraway in F. Scott Fitzgerald's *The Great Gatsby* are 'fringe narrators' of this kind. They stand as the reader's representative in the action, allowing for a focus on the story from within. Every event is filtered through their consciousness before it reaches the reader, but the narrators themselves are sufficiently detached from the action to be at least moderately trustworthy in their accounts.

Sometimes several narrators exist in the same novel, so that one narrative fits inside another like a set of Chinese boxes. This is Emily Brontë's technique in *Wuthering Heights*. There Ellen Dean the housekeeper tells the story of Wuthering Heights to Lockwood, who tells it to us. With each of them, as with all 'limited narrators', we have to ask ourselves: can we trust them? Have they any motives for distorting the story? What is their rôle in the action, and how does it affect their vision of the events?

Recent fiction has been dominated by the theory of the limited point of view. I once saw a postal course in story-writing which asserted that a change of viewpoint was an unforgivable error on the part of the author, a lapse into inconsistency which would deflect the reader's interest from the narrative altogether. But it is easy to see how this kind of fatuous and categoric statement came into being. If modern fiction has one overwhelming common theme, it is that of the conflict between the individual sensibility and the alien world outside. With such a subject only one point of view is possible—that of the sensitive, and usually suffering, hero. The modern English and American novel has proliferated into a large number of private, subjective worlds. A random count of novels published since 1920 would, I think, reveal a disproportionately frequent use of first-person and single-character narration.

As early as 1927, E. M. Forster complained about programmatic insistence on a limited point of view in *Aspects of the Novel*. His remarks there strike me as offering the most penetrating insight into the problem that we have:

A novelist can shift his viewpoint if it comes off, and it came off with Dickens and Tolstoy. Indeed this power to expand and contract perception (of which the shifting view-point is a symptom), this right to intermittent knowledge:—I find it one of the great advantages of the novel-form, and it has a parallel in our perception of life. We are stupider at some times than others; we can enter into people's minds occasionally but not always, because our own minds get tired; and this intermittence lends in the long run variety and colour to the experiences we receive. A quantity of novelists, English novelists especially, have behaved like this to the people in their books: played fast and loose with them, and I cannot see why they should be censured.

Forster called this technique of shifting the viewpoint 'bouncing'. In his own novels Forster gives a superb demonstration of the power and flexibility of bounced narrative, blending the possi-bilities of both omniscience and the limited point of view. He inhabits one character after another, sometimes expressing sympathy with the villain of the piece, sometimes with the hero, sometimes with the general social climate of the place and period of the novel. He is a chameleon and he rarely gives the reader an opportunity to pin him down to a consistent attitude. Anyone who has read *Howards End* will be familiar with the subtle ambiguity of Forster's moral sympathies. Is the ending of that novel really as optimistic as it appears to be on the surface? What does Forster really think of Helen Schlegel or Leonard Bast? The questions are as arguable as they were when the book was written. In bounced narrative the reader has to make up his own mind about the characters. It forms the natural method for the ironist who wishes to allow distinctions of character to speak for themselves. At the same time, it demands of the reader that he comply with the suggestion Henry James made to the aspiring novelist: 'Try to be one of those upon whom nothing is lost.'

## ROSE LORIMER AND CLARISSA CRANE
from *Anglo-Saxon Attitudes* by Angus Wilson

Rose Lorimer, struggling with weighed-down shopping baskets, made her immense way among the marble and mosaic of the Corner House, caught a passing view of herself in a mirror and was pleased. She had always affirmed that women scholars were primarily women and should not disregard the demands of feminine fashion. To advertise learning by disregard of dress was to be odd, and Dr. Lorimer disliked oddity more than anything. The vast intellectual excitement of her researches since the war had not left her a lot of time for thinking about clothes, but her mother had always said that with a good fur coat, however old, one could not go wrong; and for her own part, she had added a bold dash of colour to cheer our drab English winter—woman's contribution to banish gloom. Twenty years ago, of course, she reflected, straw hats with flowers would have been out of place in December, but the dictates of fashion were so much less strict nowadays, it seemed. And then Dr. Lorimer had always loved artificial flowers, especially roses.

There was no want of artificial flowers in the Corner House entrance hall. An enormous cardboard turkey and an enormous cardboard goose, owing their inspiration to somewhat vulgarized memories of Walt Disney, held between them the message MERRY XMAS made entirely of white and pink satin roses. As the tableau revolved, the turkey changed to a Christmas pudding and the goose to a mince pie, each suitably adorned with a wide grin and two little legs; AND A PROSPEROUS NEW YEAR they announced, this time in real chrysanthemums. Dr. Lorimer thought amusedly of Christmas, so rich in pagan symbols; the Real Masters of the Church had taken small pains to disguise their victory there. Muffled voices at the back of her mind pressed her to change her tense—*take* small pains, it said. In two days' time, she thought, Initiates everywhere—in northern Europe, and farther even than that—will be working their old magical spells of health and renewal over their unsuspecting Christian flocks. In England here, their archbishop—King Fisher—she smiled to think of the significance of the name, would be at the head of them. So old a mystery concealed for so long from so many, but not from her. She shook herself and drove off the voices. Knowledge led one into such strange dreams. It was all over long ago, of course. Nevertheless, the early Christian missionaries bought their pagan converts at high price with the ceremonial adulteration of their Saviour's birthday.

She tucked her giant legs with difficulty beneath one of the small tables and looked at the menu with a certain puritan alarm at its luxurious array of dishes. Choice was made simpler for one, she reflected, at her usual 'ordinary' Lyons or A.B.C. She sighed at the uneasy prospect of sensual choice. Clarissa Crane, however, appeared to be such a distinguished novelist, and novelists, no doubt, were used to living luxuriously. A few years ago she would not have imagined herself introducing a novelist as a guest at the Annual Lecture, but Miss Crane's letter had sounded so very interested; and if the academical world insisted on its narrow limits, then other means of disseminating the truth must be found.

Clarissa Crane, searching the vast marble tea-room with a certain distaste, suddenly recognized her learned hostess and felt deeply embarrassed. In all this drab collection of matinée-goers and pantomime parties, that only could be her. She had expected somebody dowdy, indeed had worn her old green tweed suit in deference to the academic occasion, but she had not been prepared for someone quite so outrageously odd, so completely a 'fright'. Dr. Lorimer was mountainous, not only up and down, but round and round as well, and then her clothes were so strange—that old, old fur coat, making almost no pretence of the large safety-pins that held it together, and, above the huge aimlessly smiling grey face, a small toque composed entirely of artificial pink roses and set askew on a bundle of tumbling black coils and escaping hairpins. Clarissa, with a sensitive novelist's eye dreaded to think into what strange realm the poor creature's mind had strayed; with a woman of the world's tact, however, she cried, 'Dr. Lorimer, this is so awfully kind of you!'

'Not at all, dear, I was only too glad to be of help. It's so seldom that Clio can aid the other muses, isn't it?' Dr. Lorimer's voice was strangely small coming out of her massive form, like a little girl's reciting a party piece. Its childish effect was the greater after Clarissa Crane's sophisticated, strangled contralto: 'I do hope I can help you,' Rose said, 'because your novel sounds so very, very interesting.' Her mind strayed away over the novels *she* had read—*The Forsyte Saga*, *The Last Days of Pompeii* a book called *Beau Sabreur*, and, of course, a number more when she was a girl. *They* hadn't been interesting at all, she remembered.

'Thank you,' said Clarissa, 'I'm sure you can. Taking me to this frightfully important lecture in itself, and then, I wanted to know . . .'

Rose Lorimer interrupted her question, 'We'd better choose something to eat, dear, first,' she said, and looked at Clarissa over the top of the menu with a sort of shy leer. She was not normally given to calling people 'dear' or to leering at them, but she had somehow arrived at this approach as suitable for so unusual a companion as a smart lady novelist. It was a manner that recalled a poor stage performance of a bawd and suggested a sub-conscious appraisal of her guest that was hardly complimentary. 'Will you have an ice, dear?' she asked, and then, remembering the seasonable cold weather, she added, 'or there seems to be sundries,' and she lingered over the wondrous range of dishes in print before her.

'Oh, no, just some tea,' Clarissa said, and then fearing to hurt the poor creature's feelings, added, 'and some toast would be nice.'

'Toast,' repeated Rose. 'What with, dear?'

'Oh, just butter.' Clarissa feared being involved with sardines.

'I don't see toast and *butter*,' said Rose, who *had* in fact got involved with the sardine section, 'Oh, yes, I do. It's farther down. *Buttered* toast,' she explained.

'Of course, I've no right at all to consider doing a *historical* novel,' said Clarissa, her eye trying to avoid the glistening circle of butter-grease that grew ever larger around Dr. Lorimer's lips. 'But somehow I feel the past speaks for us so much at this moment.' It was the critics, in fact, who had spoken so determinedly against her knowledge of modern life in her last novel. 'And then those extraordinary dark centuries, the faint twilight that flickers around the departing Romans and the real Arthur, the strange shapes thrown up by the momentary gleams of our knowledge, and, above all, the enormous sense of its relation to ourselves, its nowness, if I can call it that. The brilliant Romano-British world, the gathering shadows, and then the awful darkness pouring in.'

Rose, who, when the muffled voices of her *idées fixes* were not working in her, was a very down-to-earth scholar, could make nothing of all this darkness and light business. She contented herself with eating as much of the buttered toast as possible; then, taking out a packet of Woodbines, she lit one and blew a cloud of smoke in Clarissa's direction, as though she was smoking out a nest of wasps. 'I'm afraid you won't find much of all that in Pforzheim's lecture, dear,' she said kindly; 'it's about trade.'

ANALYSIS

Rose Lorimer and Clarissa Crane represent two very different social categories: the female scholar and the woman of fashion. The gulf of ignorance and incomprehension which separates them is unbridgeable. Wilson appropriately makes them meet in Lyons Corner House, a neat touch, since neither of them is at home in that modern social melting-pot. All of Wilson's writing here is directed towards generating the sense of embarrassment occasioned by the women's awkward meeting, and he exploits the advantages of an extremely flexible narrative technique. In E. M. Forster's phrase, he 'plays fast and loose' with his characters. During the episode we are made aware of three points of view: that of Rose, that of Clarissa, and that of some discreet and perceptive observer—the detached viewpoint of Wilson and his readers as they overhear the encounter.

Both characters are 'interiorized': that is to say, the author allows himself the liberty of knowing what they are thinking and feeling. Consider the way in which Wilson treats Dr. Lorimer: the opening sentence betrays an interesting shift of viewpoint.

> Rose Lorimer, struggling with weighed-down shopping baskets, made her immense way among the marble and mosaic of the Corner House, caught a passing view of herself in a mirror and was pleased.

The first half of the sentence presents Rose seen from a distance. She would hardly be likely to think of herself as 'making her immense way', and the phrase is obviously coined by an observer of the scene (it might of course be made by Clarissa Crane). But by the time that Rose has reached the mirror, Wilson has jumped *inside* his character, giving us her view of things. For the whole of the first three paragraphs the viewpoint is largely Rose's own, although Wilson does punctuate the narrative with occasional sentences which describe Rose from outside. Wilson temporarily adopts Rose Lorimer's point of view by appropriating her own vocabulary and style of expression. Rose has a good deal of brash assurance and her manner is reflected in the words she uses. The cumulative effect of phrases like 'She had always affirmed that . . . disliked oddity . . . she had added a bold dash of colour to cheer our drab English winter . . . had always loved artificial flowers' is to convey a sense of Rose's enthusiasm and assertive, if faintly eccentric, taste.

When Wilson deals with Clarissa Crane he equips her with an interior vocabulary which sharply contrasts with that of Rose Lorimer. Clarissa's 'certain distaste . . . deference to the academic occasion . . . sensitive novelist's eye . . . woman of the world's tact' emphasizes her conscious reserve in the face of Rose's boldness. At the same time, her language reveals a degree of naïve romanticism: she 'dreaded to think into what strange realm the poor creature's mind had strayed'. Her sensitivity, too, degenerates into a comic priggishness: she 'feared being involved with sardines'.

Clarissa's 'fear' ('fear', 'dread' and 'alarm' are key words in her vocabulary) gives her an area of common ground with Rose, since Rose too is 'alarmed' at the menu, at the 'uneasy prospect of sensual choice'. This is where much of the comedy of Wilson's bounced narrative emerges: we see both characters from the inside, are aware of the trepidation of both of them, and are equally conscious of the fact that neither has a clue as to how the other is thinking.

The whole episode is a drama of misunderstanding, of which a cross-section has been delicately opened to the reader's gaze. In the second paragraph for instance, we are invited to share Rose Lorimer's amusement at the anthropological implications of Christmas festivities. The joke is a subtle one and merits Dr. Lorimer's smile as she walks across the tea-room. But during the fourth paragraph, as we watch Rose through the eyes of Clarissa Crane, we are asked to accept a description of her which includes her 'aimlessly smiling grey face'. We immediately have to refocus any growing sympathy for Clarissa, for here she is factually in error: Rose's smile is far from being 'aimless'.

The matter comes up again towards the end of the extract, when Clarissa lectures Rose on 'the darkness and light business'. Miss Crane lacks the advantage of the reader who has shared Rose's reflections on the tawdry Christmas decorations. When Clarissa observes that 'the past speaks for us so much at this moment', she launches into a vague rhapsodic account of the coming of the dark ages. Rose, for whom the past genuinely does speak—as the artificial flowers, the turkey and the goose evidence a survival of pagan symbolism—is justifiably nonplussed. To the reader, confronted on the one hand with Clarissa Crane's fashionable gush, and on the other with Rose Lorimer's substantial knowledge, insight and humour, the victory goes rather surprisingly, and on points, to the mountainous Dr. Lorimer.

But throughout the extract Angus Wilson does more than bounce us from inside one character to inside the other. Midway through the passage there is a characteristic moment:

> Dr. Lorimer's voice was strangely small coming out of her massive form, like a little girl's reciting a party piece. Its childish effect was the greater after Clarissa Crane's sophisticated, strangled contralto.

During these two sentences we are distanced from both characters. The effect is as if the novelist had suddenly moved us to some vantage point on the far side of the café: the point of view is now independent of characterization, the writer is speaking for himself, and for us. Such intermittent detachment enables us to see the characters as essentially pathetic, caught in a dance which is as comic to the outsider as it is humiliating to the characters themselves. Yet the interiorization of much of the narrative never allows us completely to lose sympathy with either Dr. Lorimer or Miss Crane.

Angus Wilson has frequently argued that the modern novel must regain the breadth and variety of the great novels of the nineteenth century. Technically, Wilson is almost alone among contemporary authors in the versatile traditionalism of his technique. His broad conception of narrative, with its allowance of shifting viewpoints and rich ironic contrasts, is entirely consistent with his view of the art of the novelist. In Wilson's own words:

> Like any other artist's, the novelist's statement is a concentrated vision; he aims as much as any symbolist poet or impressionist painter at seizing the 'stuff' of life and communicating it totally; but, unlike the others he has chosen the most difficult of all forms, one that makes its own discipline as it goes along.

## 3 Narrative: Dramatized Consciousness

There is one variety of single-character narration which should be considered independently in some detail. The publication of Mark Twain's *Huckleberry Finn* in the United States in 1885, and of James Joyce's *Ulysses* in Paris and London in 1922, afford two seminal dates for the historian of modern fiction. In both novels the narrative was a dramatization in language of the workings of the central character's consciousness. His vocabulary and syntax reflected his interior processes of perception, thought and speech. The techniques of 'vernacular narrative' and of 'stream of consciousness' treat language dynamically: they catch it in the act of being formed, and respect it as offering a unique version both of the consciousness of the hero and of the outlines of his world. The American anthropologist Ashley Montagu has commented that, 'Every language enshrines its own reality, for the world is organized according to the manner reflected in the language.' Twain and Joyce explored the particular realities enshrined in the speech of Huck Finn's Missouri and the Blooms' Dublin.

I knowed I was all right now. Nobody else would come a-hunting after me. I got my traps out of the canoe and made me a nice camp in the thick woods. I made a kind of a tent out of my blankets to put my things under so the rain couldn't get at them. I catched a cat-fish and haggled him open with my saw, and towards sundown I started my camp-fire and had supper. Then I set out a line to catch some fish for breakfast.

When it was dark I set by my camp-fire smoking, and feeling pretty satisfied; but by-and-by it got sort of lonesome,

and so I went and set on the bank and listened to the currents
washing along, and counted the stars and drift-logs and rafts
that come down, and then went to bed; there ain't no better
way to put in time when you are lonesome; you can't stay so,
you soon get over it.

Huck Finn speaking. The whole of Twain's novel is presented
as if it was spoken by Huck himself. There are important
consequences here for the nature of narrative: no feeling can be
expressed, nor event analysed, unless it comes within the range
of Huck's limited command of grammar and vocabulary. Look
at the way in which Huck records his actions in the first paragraph: one succeeds another like items in a shopping list. Huck's
characteristic syntactical structure is the simple sentence in which
connections are made by the use of 'and' or 'then'. He never
superimposes an adult logic on his actions and rarely presses an
interpretation of events on to the reader. When things happen
in *Huckleberry Finn*, Huck notes them down faithfully and
factually, never using intellect to distort or justify them. His
consciousness is empty of presuppositions about the world and
his narrative dramatically enacts his innocence. When he
expresses his feelings, too, a comparable process takes place.
Huck indicates rather than explains his responses: 'By-and-by it
got sort of lonesome.'—We know what he means and fill in the
details for ourselves. In the conventional literary narrative, of
course, the nature of Huck's loneliness would be probed and
illustrated in detail. Twain's vernacular narrative cleaves to
Huck's own resources of language and in the process exactly
recreates the quality of Huck's own sensibility.

Just as Twain seizes on language at the moment that it becomes
speech, so Joyce catches it seconds earlier, as fragments of words
and sentences run through the mind of someone thinking. Here
are the opening few lines of Molly Bloom's monologue at the
end of *Ulysses*:

Yes because he never did a thing like that before as ask to get his breakfast in bed with a couple of eggs since the *City Arms* hotel when he used to be pretending to be laid up with a sick voice doing his highness to make himself interesting to that old faggot Mrs Riordan that he thought he had a great leg of and she never left us a farthing all for masses for herself and her soul greatest miser ever was actually afraid to lay out 4d for her methylated spirit telling me all her ailments she had too much chat in her about politics and earthquakes and the end of the world let us have a bit of fun first God help the world if all the women were her sort down on bathingsuits and lownecks . . .

Molly Bloom's 'stream of consciousness' continues like this for sixty-one pages without a punctuation mark. For thought itself is subject to no grammatical rules: it shifts from one perception to another effortlessly. Images are abruptly broken off and new ones take their place. We move from Mr. Bloom's breakfast in bed to Mrs. Riordan's stinginess, and on through the whole of Molly Bloom's accumulated experience, stored in her memory and available for immediate recall as soon as the right word or image appears to trigger it off. Neither formal logic nor conventional concepts of time operate in Mrs. Bloom's mind. Past and present events intermingle in her consciousness, and things happen by random association rather than by any scheme of causation. If we tend to think of the conventional narrative as an organization of events in time, then the 'stream of consciousness narrative' represents the disorganization of events out of time. The only consistent element in Molly Bloom's monologue is the continued presence of Molly herself. The narrative is a working-model of her consciousness.

The work of both Twain and Joyce still strongly influences modern writers. In America the vernacular narrative has become established as a central literary tradition. In the nineteen-twenties Sherwood Anderson, Ernest Hemingway and Ring Lardner all adapted the vocabulary and inflections of Middle-Western speech as a literary medium. In Lardner's stories the narrators are often illiterates, who speak with an uneducated and vivid fluency, but who write in a mixture of stilted, misspelt formality and snappy colloquialism:

> Wed. Apr. 12
>
> I am 16 of age and am a caddy at the Pleasant View Golf Club but only temporary as I expect to soon land a job some wheres as asst pro as my game is good enough now to be a pro but to young looking. My pal Joe Bean also says I have not got enough swell head to make a good pro but suppose that will come in time, Joe is a wise cracker.

Lardner's bums and baseball players exemplify an important characteristic of true vernacular narrative. Since the speech of the narrator must be adequately differentiated from the 'standard language' of his place and period, the narrator must be a child or an uneducated man. In practice the vernacular narrative is generally a vehicle for an uncultivated sensibility whose very naïvete makes for a kind of wisdom. A recent vernacular narrative, J. D. Salinger's *The Catcher in the Rye*, bears out this tendency. Its hero, sixteen-year-old Holden Caulfield, discovers to his horror that he is being forcibly drawn into the adult world. All adults are 'phoneys', and Holden wilfully rejects intellectuality and grown-up behaviour on the grounds that they will automatically make him a 'phoney' too. Contemporary English 'vernacular innocents' include the teenage narrators of Stan Barstow's *A Kind of Loving* and Alan Sillitoe's *The Loneliness of the Long Distance Runner*.

The influence of Joyce's stream of consciousness has been less direct but more wholly pervasive than that of Twain's vernacular narrative. Joyce carried his technique to its farthest imaginable limits, and when it is used by more recent writers, it generally appears in a considerably modified form. William Faulkner, the American novelist, was deeply indebted to Joyce when he wrote *The Sound and the Fury* (1929). The first quarter of that novel consists of an interior monologue in the mind of an idiot who has the power of total recall, but no sense of relative time. Like Faulkner, few novelists manage to escape Joyce completely when they move inside the minds of their characters, for the stream of consciousness has provided literature with a new convention for the representation of the thinking process. When characters think, they tend to do so in the long shadow of Molly Bloom.

## HERZOG ON THE TRAIN TO MARTHA'S VINEYARD
### from *Herzog* by Saul Bellow

*Moses Herzog is a forty-seven-year-old professor of political philosophy. His second marriage has just broken up, and he is left with a derelict country mansion, several friends and two mistresses. During the novel he is always on the move, turning events over in his head, writing imaginary letters to both the living and the dead. Here he is en route to stay with friends: his train has just left Grand Central Station, New York.*

. . . Herzog broke off. A dining-car steward rang the chimes for lunch, but Herzog had no time to eat. He was about to begin another letter.

*Dear Professor Byzhkovski, I thank you for your courtesy in Warsaw. Owing to the state of my health, our meeting must have been unsatisfactory to you.* I sat in his apartment making paper hats and boats out of the *Trybuna Ludu* while he tried to get a conversation going. The professor—that tall powerful man in a sandy-tweed shooting costume of knickers and Norfolk jacket—must have been astonished. I'm convinced he has a kind nature. His blue eyes are the good sort. A fat but shapely face, thoughtful and manly. I kept folding the paper hats—I must have been thinking of the children. Mme. Byzhkovski asked me did I want jam in my tea, bending over hospitably. The furniture was richly polished, old, of a vanished Central European epoch—but then this present epoch is vanishing, too, and perhaps faster than all the others. *I hope you will forgive me. I have now had an opportunity to read your study of the American Occupation of West Germany. Many of the facts are disagreeable.* But I was never consulted by President Truman, nor by Mr. McCloy. *I must confess I haven't examined the German question as closely as I should. None of the governments are truthful, in my opinion. There is also an East German question not even touched upon in your monograph.*

I wandered in Hamburg into the red-light district. That is, I was told that I should see it. Some of the whores, in black lace underthings, wore German military boots and rapped at you with riding crops on the windowpanes. Broads with red complexions, calling and grinning. A cold, joyless day.

*Dear Sir*, wrote Herzog. *You have been very patient with the Bowery bums who enter your church, pass out drunk, defecate in the pews, break bottles on the gravestones, and commit more nuisances. I would suggest that as you can see Wall Street from your church door you might prepare a pamphlet to explain that the Bowery gives additional significance to it. Skid Row is the contrasting institution, therefore necessary. Remind them of Lazarus and Dives. Because of Lazarus, Dives gets an extra kick, a bonus, from his luxuries.* No, I don't believe Dives is having such a hot time, either. And if he wants to free himself, the doom of Skid Row awaits him. If there were a beautiful poverty, a moral poverty in America, that would be subversive. Therefore it has to be ugly. Therefore the bums are working for Wall Street—confessors of the name. But the Reverend Beasley, where does he get his dough?

*We have thought too little on this.*

He then wrote, *Credit Department, Marshall Field & Co. I am no longer responsible for the debts of Madeleine P. Herzog. As of March 10, we ceased to be husband and wife. So don't send me any* more bills—*I was knocked over by the last—more than four hundred dollars. For purchases made after the separation. Of course I should have written sooner—to what is called the credit nerve-centre—Is there such a thing? Where can you find it?—but I temporarily lost my bearings.*

*Dear Professor Hoyle, I don't think I understand just how the Gold-Pore Theory works. How the heavier metals—iron, nickel—get to the centre of the earth, I think I see. But what about the concentration of lighter metals? Also, in your explanation of the formation of smaller planets,* including our tragic earth, *you speak of adhesive materials that bind the agglomerates of precipitated matter. . . .*

The wheels of the cars stormed underneath. Woods and pastures ran up and receded, the rails of sidings sheathed in rust, the dipping racing wires, and on the right the blue of the Sound, deeper, stronger than before. Then the enamelled shells of the commuters' cars, and the heaped bodies of junk cars, the shapes of old New England mills with narrow, austere windows; villages, convents; tugboats moving in the swelling fabric-like water; and then plantations of pine, the needles on the ground of a life-giving russet colour. So, thought Herzog, acknowledging that his imagination of the universe was elementary, the novae bursting and the worlds coming into being, the invisible magnetic spokes by means of which bodies kept one another in orbit. Astronomers made it all sound as though the gases were shaken up inside a flask. Then after many billions of years, light-years, this childlike but far from innocent creature, a straw hat on his head, and a heart in his breast, part pure, part wicked, who would try to form his own shaky picture of this magnificent web.

*Dear Dr. Bhave,* he began again, *I read of your work in the* Observer *and at the time thought I'd like to join your movement. I've always wanted very much to lead a moral, useful, and active life. I never knew where to begin. One can't become Utopian. It only makes it harder to discover where your duty really lies. Persuading the owners of large estates to give up some land to impoverished peasants, however.* . . . These dark men going on foot through India. In his vision Herzog saw their shining eyes, and the light of spirit within them. You must start with injustices that are obvious to everybody, not with big historical perspectives. *Recently, I saw* Pather Panchali. *I assume you know it, since the subject is rural India. Two things affected me greatly—the old crone scooping the mush with her fingers and later going into the weeds to die; and the death of the young girl in the rains.* Herzog, almost alone in the Fifth Avenue Playhouse, cried with the child's mother when the hysterical death music started. Some musician with a native brass horn, imitating sobs, playing a death noise. It was raining also in New York, as in rural India. His heart was aching. He too had a daughter, and his mother too had been a poor woman. He had slept on sheets made of flour sacks. The best type for the purpose was Ceresota.

What he had vaguely in mind was to offer his house and property in Ludeyville to the Bhave movement. But what could Bhave do with it? Send Hindus to the Berkshires? It wouldn't be fair to them. Anyway, there was a mortgage. A gift should be made in what they call 'fee simple', and for that I'd have to raise another eight thousand bucks, and the Internal Revenue wouldn't give me a deduction on it. Foreign charities probably don't count. Bhave would be doing him a favour. That house was one of his biggest mistakes. It was bought in a dream of happiness, an old ruin of a place but with enormous possibilities— great old trees, formal gardens he could restore in his spare time. The place had been deserted for years. Duck hunters and lovers would break in and use it; and when Herzog posted the property the lovers and the hunters played jokes on him. Someone came in the night and left a used sanitary napkin in a covered dish on his desk, where he kept bundles of notes for his Romantic studies. That was his reception by the natives. A momentary light of self-humour passed over his face as the train flashed through meadows and sunny pines. Suppose I accepted the challenge. I could be Moses, the old Jew-man of Ludeyville, with a white beard, cutting the grass under the washline with my antique reel-mower. Eating woodchucks.

ANALYSIS

*Herzog* is a kind of patchwork quilt of all the ideas, memories, speculations and perceptions which engross the hero during the course of the novel. Bellow's writing blends both vernacular and stream of consciousness traditions. But what is entirely new in American fiction is that Bellow's central character is an intellectual (though a comically failed intellectual) and the consciousness dramatized in the narrative is the consciousness of a man of ideas. Herzog thinks and feels with frenzied articulacy, and Bellow's novel charts every shift and twist of his mind.

A brief paraphrase of the passage sharply reveals its profuse complexity. An imaginary letter to a German scholar on a political question shifts to memories of the scholar's family, back to the politics of a divided country, on to Herzog's memories of the red-light district in Hamburg, to Skid Row (and another letter), to questions of the use of capital, to a letter to the credit-department of a store where his ex-wife has an account in his name. The phrase 'nerve-centre' moves Herzog on to astronomy and a letter to Fred Hoyle. While speculating on the universe, Herzog suddenly becomes aware of the present moment, of the landscape speeding past the train window, then switches back to his own position and responsibility in space and time. This leads him to a new letter, this time to an Indian philanthropist, and memories of a film of poverty in India. He recalls that he has slept on Indian sacks and thinks of offering his country house to the Bhave movement. This raises questions of law, taxation and real-estate, then sends Herzog scuttling back to a vision of pastoral harmony, with Herzog as primitive rural settler.

All this in just over one thousand words. Herzog's transitions of thought are as rapid and as loosely associative as those of Molly Bloom. Memories of the past, speculations about the future and worries of the present mix in Herzog's brain. He skids off the present moment at a tangent: we are given one brief glimpse of what is happening outside while Herzog sits in the train, before being flung again into the timeless jumble of Herzog's consciousness. One idea breeds another in a relentless process of evolution and Herzog is held captive by his own imagination.

Herzog's jumble of ideas is correlated by his jumble of vernacular idioms. He contains within himself at least four 'characters': the private citizen, the intellectual, the moral preacher and the man of affairs. Each of Herzog's *personae* has his own peculiar jargon, and a switch of thought entails a switch of language. Notice such transitions as this one:

> If there were a beautiful poverty, a moral poverty in America, that would be subversive. Therefore it has to be ugly. Therefore the bums are working for Wall Street—confessors of the name. But the Reverend Beasley, where does he get his dough?
> *We have thought too little on this.*
> He then wrote, *Credit Department, Marshall Field & Co. I am no longer responsible for the debts of Madeleine P. Herzog. As of March 10, we ceased to be husband and wife.*

Herzog's easy, colloquial moralism changes without warning into the stilted formality of the business-letter. Bellow is adept at catching the exact tone of personal reminiscence or engaged intellectual argument: he is constantly changing gear throughout the novel, so that Herzog exhibits a conglomeration of styles to match the variety of his obsessions. There are moments when, off-guard, Herzog sounds like a traditional vernacular narrator, simple, slangy and fluent ('I kept folding the paper hats—I must have been thinking of the children. Mme. Byzhkovski asked me did I want jam in my tea—'). There are others when Herzog's voice takes on the tone of an Old Testament prophet, or a dry scholar. Bellow makes free with his pronouns, and the narrative zigzags from the first to the third person, allowing an additional varying factor in the composition of the language of the book. But we are always conscious of Herzog talking to himself in an endless and variegated interior monologue.

Saul Bellow himself has said of *Herzog*:

> The point of the book is that here is a man who having led the life of an intellectual in the United States finds that it was highly unsatisfactory, to say the least; that he pursued happiness after the fashion of educated Americans; that it thrust him into the isolation of a private life which brought him nothing but shame and humiliation; and that he, precisely he, was the man who lacked the kind of true knowledge which might have brought him into useful contact with other human beings.

In the novel there is no real consistency of time, logic or language. Herzog is a fragmented man, splintered into facets which will not fit together into a unified whole. Intellect, emotion and perception are at war, and Herzog's tragedy is the loss of control and direction. Bellow's vision of the life of an intellectual in America is one of massive personal disintegration. His triumph as a novelist is to have turned that disintegration into the backbone of his literary form.

## 4   Narrative: Time

No narrative exists that does not create some kind of time scheme. For E. M. Forster, in *Aspects of the Novel*, there was a clock ticking away in every piece of fiction: some writers speeded this clock up, some slowed it down, some set the hands back or forward, but none were able to abolish the clock altogether. At the same time, the novelist is in a special sense answerable to history: his story is located within a particular area of time, and every detail of the décor, every snatch of dialogue, every action of the characters, must be appropriate to the period in which the novel is set. It is useful to distinguish these two related aspects of the topic, for every novel is both 'an organization of events in time' and 'a piece of history'. One could label the two functions 'the micro-narrative' and 'the macro-narrative'—the time-scheme within the novel and the relationship that that small structure bears to the larger perspective of history.

In selecting his time scheme the novelist is faced with a choice between three basic alternatives. He may aim for an Aristotelian 'unity of time', so that the events of the novel are transacted in roughly the same time as it takes to read the book. Both Christopher Isherwood's *A Single Man* and James Joyce's *Ulysses* deal with a day in the lives of their characters, enforcing an approximate correspondence between 'reading time' and 'acting time'. Or the novelist may decide to contract and summarize time, allowing many years to elapse between his first and last pages. But either choice will be modified by the third alternative, for narrative, however primarily conceived, mixes its times kaleidoscope-fashion. The simplest narrative is likely to blend the processes of perception, memory and speculation. Consider this sentence:

> As he sat in the taxi, the memory of his failure last week was strong in him: today's interview could be at least no worse than that.

One of the functions of the storyteller is to be everywhere at the same time, mindful of past history, conscious of the present and aware of the possibilities of the future. In his narrative all known or expected time can be brought to focus on the immediate event, and in the process the 'novelist's clock' is made to tell different times simultaneously.

Some formal categories of fiction create their own distinctive time schemes. The 'history' or 'chronicle' (Trollope's *Barsetshire Chronicles*, Galsworthy's *The Forsyte Saga*, Anthony Powell's *The Music of Time* series) deals with many years of change and development in the lives of a large group of characters. The 'anecdote' (many short stories fall into this class) seizes upon a single illuminating incident that may take only minutes to enact. The 'journal' (Gogol's *Diary of a Madman*, Sartre's *La Nausée*) consists of a day-to-day commentary by a single character on the events of a period. The 'assembled evidence of witnesses' (William Faulkner's *As I Lay Dying*, Julian Mitchell's *Imaginary Toys*) is made up of a series of individual accounts of the same incidents, in which the reader is repeatedly sent back to the beginning of the story, each time from a different character's point of view.

One of the ways in which the narrator can order a story is by varying the proportion of time allocated to particular incidents. An important event can be described at greater length than it took to happen, while a whole swathe of history may be dealt with in a paragraph. This flexibility of tempo is one of the novelist's major instruments: he can indicate the relative value of each occurrence by his handling of pace. The Synoptic

Gospels afford striking examples of differences in narrative speed: when Saint Matthew, Saint Mark and Saint Luke describe the same occasion they often vary tremendously in the amount of narrative time that they allow it. Here, for example, are the accounts of Saint Matthew and Saint Mark of Christ's healing of the boy with a dumb spirit:

*Saint Mark, ix, v. 25–27*
And when Jesus saw that a multitude came running together, he rebuked the unclean spirit, saying unto him, Thou dumb and deaf spirit, I command thee, come out of him, and enter no more into him. And having cried out and torn him much, he came out: and the child became as one dead; insomuch that the more part said, He is dead. But Jesus took him by the hand, and raised him up; and he arose.

*Saint Matthew, xvii, v. 18*
And Jesus rebuked him

And the devil went out from him: and the boy was cured from that hour.

As here, narrative tempo is largely determined by the amount of detail. But syntax too has an important part to play. Short clauses, strung together with connectives like 'and' or 'then' tend to convey an impression of greater speed than elaborate dependent constructions. A recurrent item in Saint Mark's vocabulary is the word 'straightway', which he uses frequently to remind the reader of the rapid succession of the events he is describing.

But all these structures and devices must be tested in the light of the 'macro-narrative', where the novel is located in terms of historical actuality and possibility. The adage that literature deals with 'the perennial problems of humanity' is only a half-truth, at least in so far as it is applied to fiction. For the novel deals with society, and as society changes its technology and its manners, so the individual sensibility is changed too. As Marx observed, 'It is not the consciousness of men that determines their being, but, on the contrary, their social being determines their consciousness.' Conceptions of character and behaviour are grounded in history, and fiction—more than any other literary form—expresses the interdependence of person, time and place. The American critic Lionel Trilling once wrote of the way in which a culture has 'a hum and buzz of implication': that hum and buzz provides the novelist with his chosen territory.

On the simplest level, we demand that a novel offer an 'authentic' version of reality. Nothing must happen in it that could not be imagined to occur at the time and place of the novel's setting. James Joyce, whose painstaking concern for documentary detail led him to hoard theatre programmes, ticket stubs and other minutiae as essential source material, wrote to his aunt while he was working on *Ulysses* asking her to ascertain the exact number of steps between the street and the front door of a particular Dublin house. Joyce's scrupulosity was more of a personal foible rather than an artistic necessity, but it does exemplify the inherently fact-based nature of fiction. Language, manners, architecture and the like must be consonant with the 'real' place and time of the novel. In a contemporary novel it might be entirely appropriate to make a retired air-force officer express himself in war-time slang, but if his teenage son goes round exclaiming 'bang on!' we shall find him distinctly odd. A difference of only one generation reveals major changes of cultural style and the novelist must keep his ear tuned to such patterns of cultural obsolescence and innovation.

But history does not merely furnish the novel with documentary décor; it frequently provides a model for the narrative. Fiction deals most typically with private lives, but on occasions the private transactions of a novel form part of a public historical event. Dickens' *Tale of Two Cities* dealt with the impact of the French Revolution on the lives of private citizens; John Steinbeck's

Joad family in *The Grapes of Wrath* are representative of the thousands of Oklahomans who migrated to the richer lands of California during the Depression. Iris Murdoch, in *The Red and the Green*, shows an Anglo-Irish family divided by the Easter Revolution. In these novels the timing of the narrative is acutely balanced between the demands of history on the one hand and the private, interior time scheme on the other.

### AFTER THE BLITZ

from *The Emperor of Ice Cream* by Brian Moore

*The setting of the novel is Belfast in 1940–1941. Gavin Burke is seventeen and engaged in an adolescent tussle with his father, a traditionalist, a professional lawyer and a Hitler sympathizer. At the outbreak of war Gavin left school to join a first-aid post of the A.R.P. much against the wishes of his father, and at the climax of the novel Gavin is caught up in the first air raid on Belfast. His initiation into the violence of war marks his sudden emergence into maturity. In the last pages of the novel Gavin returns to the blitzed shell of his home in the suburbs.*

1    The house was very cold. Moonlight came in through the broken windows of the dining room, striking down on the dining room table, showing slivers of glass and dust on its surface. He turned back into the blackness of the hall, forgot the step down into the kitchen and stumbled when he met it. The kitchen was moonlit, and, looking out of the shattered window at the silent, empty back yard, he wondered if there were people in any of the other houses in the avenue. Had everyone gone away? Mr. Hamilton, the dentist next door, was a staunch Churchill man, not likely to run. But still, there was a haunted, empty silence all around. He turned, found the cupboard and the candles, and carefully lit his last match.

2    He dripped hot wax from a candle end on to the kitchen table and anchored the candle in it. The candle flame cowered from

the cold wind at the window. Lighting two fresh candles, he went out of the kitchen and began to climb the stairs. At the turn of the stairs leading to the breakfast room, his father's favourite print, a framed engraving of the Parthenon, had fallen, face down, its glass shattered. Hot candle wax dripped on his fingers. He was reminded of books he had read: a boy alone, holding a candle in either hand, going upstairs in a haunted house. Yet this house was not haunted. Its dangers were real. The sirens had not sounded yet, but Lord Haw-Haw had spoken. Somewhere, above the clouds, the bombers roared over the Continent, coming in for the kill.

3    The window in the breakfast room was not broken. Dicky-Bird's cage was gone. His family had not forgotten the canary in their flight across a neutral border. He thought of his father—was it only seven months ago—sitting there, below Dicky-Bird's cage, his father's weary blue eyes, forgiving yet not forgiving, his father announcing that he, Gavin, a stupid boy, was only fit for some minor rôle in this, the grown-ups' world. Dicky-Bird sang, applauding his father's decision. Gavin turned away.

4    He went up a second flight of stairs. There was dirt on the stair carpet, and, looking up at the ceiling, he saw a long, jagged crack in the plaster. He paused on the landing and went in at the sitting room door. On a tallboy, just inside, he picked up a silver christening mug, given to Owen by Aunt Agnes. He stuck one of the candles in this mug and placed the mug on a Sheraton table near the window. Almost at once, a whistle blew in the street below. A voice called out. 'Hey, you. Put that light out.'

5    He looked through the broken window pane and saw a warden standing in the middle of the avenue, a stout elderly man, the same warden who had helped him with last night's casualties. 'What are you doing there?' the warden called. 'That house is condemned.'

6    *Condemned.* 'I live here,' he shouted down.

7    'Not any more, you don't. It's not safe. Put that light out and get out of there.'

8    He pulled down the blackout blinds and listened to the retreating sound of the warden's footsteps. The room was all shadows, half lit by the pale flickering light of the candles. This house is condemned.

9    He went towards the fireplace, holding a candle aloft and, in the round looking-glass, saw himself, dirty and strange, his steel helmet askew. In that world, encircled by the looking-glass, he had acted and reacted, had left his mark and had, in turn, been marked. His bare knees had helped wear down the old Turkey carpet, battleground of a thousand childhood games of Snap. From that gramophone, he had heard his first record. Over his mother's writing desk, the fierce stag still peered from a dark forest glade. But the picture which had hung beside it, a framed Raphael print, had fallen behind his father's bookcase. The looking-glass room, unchanged since his childhood, had changed at last. This house is condemned.

10   Condemned, the house was his. He could sleep in any bed he chose: he could break open the dining room sideboard and drink his father's port. Yet, standing in the cowering light of the candles, he feared the house. It had died, its life had fled. The dead, their faces dirty and pale, dried blood on their lips, their bowels loose in the final spasm, sat on his mother's sofas and chairs, moved in the shadows, lay out there on the landing in a stiff jumble of arms and legs. He trembled: he could not stop the trembling.

11   And then, sudden, the sound of footsteps in the hall. He must not scream: it was the warden, come back to make sure he had gone. But it was not the warden. The step was heavy and strange: the step of the dead. It came up. It came on.

His hand, holding the candle, shook so that he had to put the candle down. He turned to face the sitting room door and, suddenly, defending himself against this unknown, ran to the fireplace and took a brass poker from the set of fire tongs. In panic, his mouth dry, he turned again to face the door.

12 His father, wearing a heavy tweed overcoat, a woollen scarf knotted around his neck, his head bare, stood for a moment in the doorway, then came forward. 'Gavin.' His father's arms were around him. His hands, holding his father's shoulders, felt those shoulders tremble. They stood for a moment, embracing, and then, with no words said, both needed to sit down. They sat, side by side, on the dusty slipcovers of the sofa.

13 'You're all right, then?' his father said.

14 'Yes, Daddy.'

15 'I went to the hospital first,' his father said. 'Nobody knew anything about you. I went to the A.R.P. place. Same thing. Then I met a fellow as I was going out to the car. He said you'd spent the day burying people. Is that right, son?'

16 'Coffining them.'

17 'O, dear God,' his father said.

18 'Did you get to Dublin, all right?'

19 'Yes. They're all with your Aunt Agnes. Did you see the Miss Dempsters' house down the street?'

20 'Yes. Daddy, why did you come back?'

21 'Why?' his father said. 'I was worried about you, that's why.'

22 In the candlelight, he saw that his father was crying. He had never seen his father cry before. Did his father know that the house was condemned, did his father know that everything had changed, that things would never be the same again? A new voice, a cold grown-up voice within him said: 'No.' His father was the child now; his father's world was dead. He looked over at the wireless set, remembering his father, ear cocked for England's troubles, pleased at news of other, faraway disasters. Forget that, the grown-up voice said. He heeded that voice, heeded it as he had never heeded the childish voices of his angels. Black Angel, White Angel: they had gone forever. His father

was crying. The voice would tell him what to do. From now on, he would know these things.

23    His father seemed aware of this change. He leaned his untidy, gray head on Gavin's shoulder, nodding, weeping, confirming. 'Oh, Gavin,' his father said. 'I've been a fool. Such a fool.'

24    The new voice counselled silence. He took his father's hand.

ANALYSIS

The narrative here is broadly structured by the historical events which determine the lives of Gavin and his father. Moore introduces a galaxy of real historical figures, movements and attitudes: Winston Churchill, Lord Haw-Haw, the A.R.P., the German offensive against Northern Ireland and the divided loyalties of the Ulstermen. These provide the content and set the pace of the macro-narrative. We are presented with an historical occasion in which two worlds collide—the ordered, genteel milieu of peace-time and the wholesale violence of war. The two worlds are embodied in the persons of Gavin and his father, and just as Gavin becomes a man when the German bombers reach Belfast, so his father loses his assurance and, in a sense, his maturity: 'His father was the child now: his father's world was dead.' The private relationship of father and son mirrors the public events of June 1941, as one age becomes obsolete and a new one is ushered in. Gavin is the 'new man', able to take violence in his stride, nerved for the collapse of cosy, pre-war society. At the beginning of the first raid, Gavin and a friend stand on a rooftop, welcoming the bombers as harbingers of a new era:

> 'Blow up City Hall.'
> 'And Queen's University.'
> 'And Harland and Wolff's.'

'Blow up the Orange Hall.'
'And the cathedral and the dean.'
'Jesus, what a show.'

On one level *The Emperor of Ice Cream* works as a document: it is shaped by a knowledge of the impact of the Second World War on two generations in Belfast, and incorporates a solid fabric of factual detail. Gavin and his father are representative figures; they voice twin moods of a period, and the dialogue between parent and child belongs as much to the history of the times as it does to the internal crises of a family.

While a sense of history controls the broad outlines of the story, the powers of memory and speculation dictate the intricate time-scheme of the narrative. The whole of the extract covers a period of minutes in Gavin's life as he walks through his bombed home. The pace of the narration is detailed, reflective and slow. Little escapes Gavin's notice and the 'reading time' of the extract is, if anything, rather longer than the 'acting time'. But during this piece we are referred, not only to the events of those few moments, but to the whole of Gavin's remembered life and his expectations of the future. The house is redolent with associations and memories, and Moore uses every object encountered there as a means of directing Gavin's thoughts backwards or forwards in time. The stairs, the birdcage, the christening mug, the mirror, evoke different periods in Gavin's life, while at the same time he is overwhelmed by the presence of the dawning future of war. The walk through the house functions as an anchor for Gavin's wandering reflections as he zigzags from the present into four other areas of time—his childhood, his adolescent quarrels with his father, the horrific experiences of the previous night when he was putting mutilated corpses into coffins, and the new world of war-time. A diagrammatic profile of the narrative showing the shifts of time reveals an interesting symmetry of structure: Gavin's excursions into the past and intimations of the future are delicately balanced against one another.

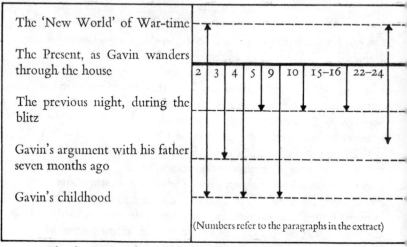

| The 'New World' of War-time | | | | | | | | |
| The Present, as Gavin wanders through the house | 2 | 3 | 4 | 5 | 9 | 10 | 15–16 | 22–24 |
| The previous night, during the blitz | | | | | | | | |
| Gavin's argument with his father seven months ago | | | | | | | | |
| Gavin's childhood | | | | | | | | |

(Numbers refer to the paragraphs in the extract)

The diagram somewhat simplifies the time scheme since Gavin's thoughts are neither as abrupt nor always quite as clear-cut as the profile would suggest. But it does indicate the range of Gavin's imagination and the evenness with which he distributes his associations over the four approximate areas of time.

The time scheme or micro-narrative acquires order and significance from the overall historical outline or macro-narrative. Gavin's thoughts are distributed on both sides of a dividing line set in 1941. The public fact of the Belfast bombing conditions the consciousness of every character in the novel. People, situations and memories are tested against a single historical criterion: do they belong to a peace-time or to a war-time world? During the book Moore explores the emergence of Gavin's characteristically post-war sensibility and maturity, and charts the decline of the comfortable middle-class verities represented by Gavin's parents, members of a smug, pre-war generation.

## 5 Narrative: Cause and Contingency

In an early chapter of John Le Carré's *The Spy who came in from the Cold* the hero, Leamas, returns home after spending the evening with his girl. The chapter ends with this paragraph:

> He left her flat and turned down the empty street towards the park. It was foggy. Some way down the road—not far, twenty yards, perhaps a bit more—stood the figure of a man in a raincoat, short and rather plump. He was leaning against the railings of the park, silhouetted in the shifting mist. As Leamas approached, the mist seemed to thicken, closing in around the figure at the railings, and when it parted the man was gone.

Because this is a spy story we know perfectly well that that lone figure in the mist is in some way connected with Leamas: he would not be there otherwise. Yet a moment's thought will remind us that the conventions of the thriller invite us to make outrageous assumptions about cause and relevance. Every clue counts: a man is shot in Bermondsey, someone is late at a party, a scientist in Copenhagen spills acid on his notes, a Mayfair flat is burgled. The apparently random paraphernalia of the mystery can all be related if only we have the key. The form of the detective or spy story works towards the revelation of that essential linking clue. But in order to follow the narrative at all, we have to take it on trust that some transcendent logic of events does exist. When reading crime fiction we would all agree with the character in Jack Gelber's play *The Connection* who observes, 'I believe it all fits together . . . we wouldn't all be on stage if it didn't.'

But does it have to fit? Roquentin, the hero of Jean-Paul Sartre's novel *La Nausée* emphatically contradicts:

> The essential thing is contingency. I mean that, by defini-
> tion, existence is not necessity. To exist is simply *to be there*;
> what exists appears, lets itself be *encountered*, but you can never
> *deduce* it. There are people, I believe, who have understood
> that. Only they have tried to overcome this contingency by
> inventing a necessary, causal being. But no necessary being can
> explain existence: contingency is not an illusion, an appear-
> ance which can be dissipated; it is absolute and consequently
> perfect gratuitousness. Everything is gratuitous, that park, this
> town, and myself.

The dialogue between Leamas and Roquentin, between the man whose world is bound by an inevitable, if incomprehensible, logic, and between the man whose world is just a bundle of unrelated coincidences, is an important one for the novelist. For a narrative conventionally consists of a series of relevant events strung on a thread of logical development. In the simple story, where our interest is sustained by the insistent question of what happens next, we demand that the storyteller keep within certain logical limits. We feel cheated if he resolves his plot by the introduction of some completely extraneous piece of information. A basic rule of the detective story is that the germ of resolution must be in the tale from the beginning. We may not have noticed the vital clue—but it must have been there. Nor is this impulse confined to the writer of thrillers. Henry James demanded that the novelist should practise a technique of 'continuous relevance', introducing nothing into his story that does not advance its logical development. And Ford Madox Ford asserted: 'Before everything a story must convey a sense of inevitability: that which happens in it must be seen to be the only thing that could have happened.'

Neither James nor Ford really faced the natural 'contingency of the novel as a form. In his recent book, *An Essay on Criticism*, Graham Hough makes a tellingly obvious, though often ignored, point: 'The novel includes more of the merely contingent, the accidental, than any other literary kind.' Hough goes on to quote from one of R. L. Stevenson's letters:

> How to get over, how to escape from, the besotting particularity of Fiction. 'Roland approached the house; it has a green door and window-blinds; and there was a scraper on the upper step.' To hell with Roland and the scraper.

The doctrine of 'continuous relevance' gets snared on the necessary descriptive detail of the novel. That door, those window-blinds, the scraper and the upper step are 'contingencies': they have no causal function in Roland's visit to the house. The novelist, as Iris Murdoch has noticed, 'has a blessed freedom from rationalism . . . he has always been . . . a describer rather than an explainer.' The novel, in its dealings with human affairs, implicitly acknowledges the place of circumstantial, though not causal, evidence. Questions of relevance are consequently very ambiguous: what is 'relevant' to a narrative includes *both* the causal *and* the contingent.

Some writers have made contingency the corner-stone of their fictional structure. Sterne, in *Tristram Shandy*, parodied the complicated plots of the novels of his day. He develops the story by means of a series of wildly unlikely coincidences, digressing at every possible opportunity to give the life history of some utterly unimportant character in minute detail. Sterne is like the teller of a shaggy dog story: he uses all the mechanics of logic and suspense to prove that, after all, there is nothing there but irrelevance and contingency.

The picaresque form of such novels as Fielding's *Tom Jones*, where the hero (classically a rogue, although the term *picaro* has passed into less precise critical usage) moves from one adventure to another, is essentially contingent. The narrative is held together, not by any scheme of logical development, but by the continuing presence and personality of the central character. Everything that happens to him, however caused, is part of the story. The old distinction between the 'novel of incident' and the 'novel of character' is a partially useful one, although it is open to dangerous simplification. The 'novel of incident' traditionally hinges on the causative development of the plot, while the 'novel of character' deals most typically with the contingencies encountered by the hero.

Contemporary novelists, particularly those who have come under the spell of existentialism, where contingency is (as it is to Roquentin) central to notions of human existence, have made use of both the Shandian and picaresque forms to come to terms with the accidental and the gratuitous. Samuel Beckett's *The Unnameable* renders the wandering consciousness of a helpless human lump, whose thoughts flicker at random around his fading field of vision. Iris Murdoch in *Under The Net* equips her free-wheeling hero with a round of fantastic adventures, each precipitated by a stroke of pure luck. John Barth (his *The End of the Road* provides the example for this chapter) has written a full-blown Shandian novel, *The Sot-Weed Factor*, an epic parody of the eighteenth-century manner in which digressions, transformation scenes and preposterous coincidences follow one another in an atmosphere of bawdy farce.

## THE PROGRESS AND ADVICE ROOM

from *The End of the Road* by John Barth

*Jacob Horner, as we later learn, met the negro Doctor by accident at the Pennsylvania Railroad Station, Baltimore. Since that morning, March 17th, 1951, the Doctor has directed Jacob's life for him. The novel opens with one of their periodic interviews.*

*In a sense, I am Jacob Horner*

It was on the advice of the Doctor that I entered the teaching profession; for a time I was a teacher of grammar at the Wicomico State Teachers College, in Maryland.

The Doctor had brought me to a certain point in my original schedule of therapies (this was in June 1953), and then, once when I drove down from Baltimore for my quarterly check-up at the Remobilization Farm, which at that time was near Wicomico, he said to me, 'Jacob Horner, you mustn't sit idle any longer. You will have to begin work.'

'I'm not idle all the time,' said I. 'I take different jobs.'

We were seated in the Progress and Advice Room of the farmhouse: there is one exactly like it in the present establishment, in Pennsylvania. It is a medium-size room, about as large as an apartment living room, only high-ceilinged. The walls are flat white, the windows are covered by white venetian blinds, usually closed, and a globed ceiling fixture provides the light. In this room there are two straight-backed white wooden chairs, exactly alike, facing each other in the centre of the floor, and no other furniture. The chairs are very close together—so close that the advisee almost touches knees with the adviser.

It is impossible to be at ease in the Progress and Advice Room. The Doctor sits facing you, his legs slightly spread, his hands on his knees, and leans a little towards you. You would not slouch down, because to do so would thrust your knees virtually against his. Neither would you be inclined to cross your legs in either the masculine or the feminine manner; the masculine manner, with your left ankle resting on your right knee, would cause your left shoe to rub against the Doctor's left trouser leg, up by his knees, and possibly dirty his white trousers; the feminine manner, with your left knee crooked over your right knee, would thrust the toe of your shoe against the same trouser leg, lower down on his shin. To sit sideways, of course, would be unthinkable, and spreading your knees in the manner of the Doctor makes you acutely conscious of aping his position, as if you hadn't a personality of your own. Your position, then (which has the appearance of choice, because you are not ordered to sit thus, but which is chosen only in a very limited sense, since there are no alternatives), is as follows: you sit rather rigidly in your white chair, your back and thighs describing the same right angle described by the structure of the chair and keep your legs together, your thighs and lower legs describing another right angle.

The placing of your arms is a separate problem, interesting in its own right and, in a way, even more complicated, but of lesser importance, since no matter where you put them they will not normally come into physical contact with the Doctor. You may do anything you like with them (you wouldn't, clearly, put them on your knees in imitation of him). As a rule I move mine about a good bit, leaving them in one position for a while and then moving them to another. Arms folded, akimbo, or dangling; hands grasping the seat edges or thighs, or clasped behind the head or resting in the lap—these (and their numerous degrees and variations) are all in their own ways satisfactory positions for the arms and hands, and if I shift from one to another, this shifting is really not so much a manifestation of embarrassment, or hasn't been since the first half-dozen interviews, as a recognition of the fact that when one is faced with such a multitude of desirable choices, no one choice seems satisfactory for very long by comparison with the aggregate desirability of all the rest, though compared to any *one* of the others it would not be found inferior.

It seems to me at just this moment (I am writing this at 7.55 in the evening of Tuesday, October 4, 1955, upstairs in the dormitory) that, should you choose to consider that final observation as a metaphor, it is the story of my life in a sentence—to be precise, in the latter member of a double predicate nominative expression in the second independent clause of a rather intricate compound sentence. You see that I was in truth a grammar teacher.

It is not fit that you should be at your ease in the Progress and Advice Room, for after all it is not for relaxation that you come there, but for advice. Were you totally at your ease, you would only be inclined to consider the Doctor's words in a leisurely manner, as one might regard the breakfast brought to one's bed by a liveried servant, hypercritically, selecting this, rejecting that, eating only as much as one chooses. And clearly such a frame of mind would be out of place in the Progress and Advice Room, for there it is you who have placed yourself in the Doctor's hands; your wishes are subservient to his, not vice versa; and his advice is given you not to be questioned or even examined (to question is impertinent; to examine, pointless), but to be followed.

'That isn't satisfactory,' the Doctor said, referring to my current practice of working only when I needed cash, and then at any job that presented itself. 'Not any longer.'

He paused and studied me, as is his habit, rolling his cigar from one side of his mouth to the other and back again, under his pink tongue.

'You'll have to begin work at a more meaningful job now. A career, you know. A calling. A lifework.'

'Yes, sir.'

'You are thirty.'

'Yes, sir.'

'And you have taken an undergraduate degree somewhere. In history? Literature? Economics?'

'Arts and sciences.'

'That's everything!'

'No major, sir.'

'Arts and sciences! What under heaven that's interesting isn't either an art or a science? Did you study philosophy?'

'Yes.'

'Psychology?'

'Yes.'

'Political science?'

'Yes.'

'Wait a minute. Zoology?'

'Yes.'

'Ah, and philology? Romance philology? And cultural anthropology?'

'Later, sir, in the graduate school. You remember, I—'

'Argh!' the Doctor said, as if hawking to spit upon the graduate school. 'Did you study lock-picking in the graduate school? Fornication? Sailmaking? Cross-examination?'

'No, sir.'

'Aren't these arts and sciences?'

'My master's degree was to be in English, sir.'

'Damn you! English *what*? Navigation? Colonial policy? Common law?'

'English literature, sir. But I didn't finish. I passed the oral examinations, but I never got my thesis done.'

'Jacob Horner, you are a fool.'

My legs remained directly in front of me, as before, but I moved my hands from behind my head (which position suggests a rather too casual attitude for many sorts of situations anyway) to a combination position, my left hand grasping my left coat lapel, my right lying palm up, fingers loosely curled, near the mid-point of my right thigh.

After a while the Doctor said, 'What reason do you think you have for not applying for a job at the little teachers college here in Wicomico?'

Instantly a host of arguments against applying for a job at the Wicomico State Teachers College presented themselves for my use, and as instantly a corresponding number of refutations lined up opposite them, one for one, so that the question of my application was held static like the rope marker in a tug-o'-war where the opposing teams are perfectly matched. This again is in a sense the story of my life, nor does it really matter if it is not just the same story as that of a few paragraphs ago: as I began to learn not long after this interview, when the schedule of therapies reached Mythotherapy, the same life lends itself to any number of stories—parallel, concentric, mutually habitant, or what you will.

Well.

'No reason, sir,' I said.

'Then it's settled. Apply at once for the fall term. And what will you teach? Iconography? Automotive mechanics?'

'English literature, I guess.'

'No. There must be a rigid discipline, or else it will be merely an occupation, not an occupational therapy. There must be a body of laws. You mean you can't teach plane geometry?'

'Oh, I suppose—' I made a suppositive gesture, which consisted of a slight outward motion of my lapel-grasping left hand, extending simultaneously the fore and index fingers but not releasing my lapel—the hand motion accompanied by quickly arched (and as quickly released) eyebrows, momentarily pursed lips, and an on-the-one-hand/on-the-other-hand rocking of the head.

'Nonsense. Of course you can't. Tell them you will teach grammar. English grammar.'

'But you know, Doctor,' I ventured, 'there is descriptive as well as prescriptive grammar. I mean, you mentioned a fixed body of rules.'

'You will teach prescriptive grammar.'

'Yes, sir.'

'No description at all. No optional situations. Teach the rules. Teach the truth about grammar.'

ANALYSIS

This heavily stylized scene establishes Jacob Horner as a victim of chance, while the Doctor plays the part of cause and logic. The dialogue between them exists almost as a series of philosophical illustrations, but Barth convincingly extends the principle of contingency into the descriptive texture of his narrative. The whole passage works as both discussion and exemplification of the conflict between cause and contingency.

Barth adopts the classic confrontation between psychiatrist and patient and turns it into a kind of metaphor. Jacob was found by the Doctor completely by chance, and since then he has never needed to make a choice for himself. He has abrogated all volition to the negro (who eventually turns out to be a criminal charlatan) and lets himself drift along whatever random route the Doctor prescribes. He has neither preference nor expectation (at one point, in a dream, Jacob rings up the meteorological office for the forecast, only to be told that tomorrow there will be no weather). As may be guessed, Jacob drifts into a situation where he destroys a marriage, a man's career and a woman's life. We leave him at the end of the novel still under the spell of the Doctor, nagged by the suspicion that maybe he does have both responsibility and choice.

'In a sense, I am Jacob Horner.'—*In a sense*, because Jacob only possesses the identity created for him by the Doctor. Is he Jacob Horner? Or is he merely an extension of the Doctor's instructions? For the Doctor personifies the principles of necessity and causality which Jacob needs in order to explain and direct his existence. The 'Progress and Advice Room' embodies the qualities of the Doctor himself: its furniture is strictly functional, arranged to impose a choiceless situation upon the interviewee:

Your position, then (which has the appearance of choice, because you are not ordered to sit thus, but which is chosen only in a very limited sense, since there are no alternatives), is as follows . . .

The Doctor's interrogation of Jacob, as he grills him about the subjects he studied at college, produces a seemingly endless list of contingencies from which a choice must be made. Every word is suspect, entailing new categories and areas of choice:

'My master's degree was to be in English, sir.'
'Damn you! English *what*? Navigation? Colonial Policy? Common Law?'

But in a contingent world of infinite combinations and possibilities, the only choice that can be valid is a negative one: 'What reason do you think you have for *not* applying for a job at the little teachers training college here in Wicomico?' Even when it has been decided that Jacob become a grammar teacher, an alarming alternative presents itself, for there is 'descriptive as well as prescriptive grammar'. The Doctor, voice of causality itself, fixes the matter. 'No description at all. No optional situations. Teach the rules.'

The peculiar strength of Barth's writing lies in the way in which contingency reasserts itself in Jacob's narration. All the time we are involved in the interview in which logic and cause win outright, we are simultaneously confronted with a world of random sensations and irrelevant speculations. 'The besotting particularity of Fiction' which bothered R. L. Stevenson, is allowed a farcical scope in *The End of the Road*:

I made a suppositive gesture, which consisted of a slight outward motion of my lapel-grasping left hand, extending simultaneously the fore and index fingers but not releasing my lapel—the hand motion accompanied by quickly arched (and as quickly released) eyebrows, momentarily pursed lips, and an on-the-one-hand/on-the-other rocking of the head.

The novel is crammed with exactitude—names, dates, places, possible alternatives, reflections which have no causal bearing on the development of the plot. For although Jacob is entirely under the direction of the Doctor, he never loses sight of all the things he might do if he were not impelled along this limited course of action. At some moments in the book, with Jacob immersed in one of his gestures, or in some trivial detail of the environment, it seems little short of miraculous that any 'story' ever emerges. But it does, though it is perpetually subject to the distorting quirks of Jacob's uncalibrated perception. Events sometimes register in minute detail, sometimes they seem to be hardly noticed at all. Barth succeeds in translating his theoretical preoccupations with contingency into the detailed fabric of language and narrative. A story for Ford Madox Ford had to convey 'a sense of inevitability': the story of *The End of the Road* conveys a sense of the merely fortuitous.

*Character*

# 6 Character and Dialogue

In fiction, as in life, our first reaction to people tends to be based on the way they talk. A voice overhead in a bus queue or supermarket, even though we may never see the speaker, can give us a clear idea of where the person comes from, what his education is, what is his likely age, and so on. An Oxford accent or a cockney whine have resonant associations with a particular class, and, by implication, with a particular character-type. When people clash, the conflict is often one of language and forms a meeting point for modes of speaking, differences of vocabulary and tones of regional and class accent. Such variations have always provided rich material for the novelist.

There is a current argument that claims the novel is dying for want of a firm fabric of social manners. As we move further away from the hierarchy imposed by an aristocratic society, say these critics, so we lose the mine of language, manners and behaviour that is the common property of a cohesive social group. Certainly things were rather more easy for the novelist in the nineteenth century: social lines were rigidly drawn and most writers felt at home in the drawing room, admired the manor and patronized the terraced house. Anthony Trollope in *Doctor Thorne* was able to establish an easy superiority over the *nouveau riche* Lady Scatcherd simply by making her exclaim 'Oh laws!' at her entrance, then speak the ' 'oo is' e?' dialect of the comic proletarian.

When the twentieth-century novelist has made his characters speak he has had to do more than sketch that simple conflict between the middle and the working classes. Our time is characterized by a social and geographic mobility that has thrown vast groups of people into amorphous national and occupational units. But mobility has also produced a complex web of specialized manners and languages. Technology, sport, academic disciplines, business concerns, particular age groups, have all created new societies with their own codes of behaviour and private jargon. In matters of education, livelihood, place of birth and social aspiration, the contemporary novelist has to 'place' his characters with a great deal of precision. 'Occupation: Gentleman' is no longer enough. The modern writer is compensated for the demands of specialization, however, by a rewarding variety of localized forms of speech. In the golf club, coffee bar or laboratory he can hear new, energetic languages going through a constant process of change and renewal.

But given this fund of raw material, the novelist must decide how to make his characters speak, and he must question what rôle he wants his dialogues to play. In *Women In Love* D. H. Lawrence gives this speech to Birkin:

> 'Right down the slopes of degeneration—mystic, universal degeneration. There are many stages of pure degradation to go through: agelong. We live on long after our death, and progressively, in progressive devolution.'

Clearly Lawrence was listening to the thought rather than the voice of Birkin. The rhythms and vocabulary of that speech are poetic and stylized, and if we try to imagine a man saying them in conversation they will sound pretentiously out of place. But Lawrence was reaching towards an operatic effect, where characters are formal mouth-pieces for sentiments and ideas larger than themselves. Tape recorder accuracy would have destroyed the impact of the idea, although it might have made Birkin more believable.

For we do not speak as we think. We talk obliquely, hinting at points, then skirting round them. The language we use is a deceptive index to what we actually feel. Hemingway realized this, and some of his bare short stories exactly catch the indirectness of speech. In 'Hills Like White Elephants' a man and a girl are waiting at a railway station. She is going away to have an abortion. The thing is never mentioned by name: it is just called 'it', and we gradually infer what is going on.

> 'If I do it you'll be happy and things will be like they were and you'll love me?'
> 'I love you now. You know I love you.'
> 'I know. But if I do it, then it will be nice again if I say things are like white elephants, and you'll like it?'
> 'I'll love it. I love it now but I just can't think about it. You know how I get when I worry.'

The author does not explain the dialogue as he goes along and the reader has to make his own response, listening and judging as he would in an actual conversation. He feels, perhaps, that the man reiterates the word 'love' rather too much, that when he says 'I'll love it. I love it now' he has accidentally tripped into an admission that he does not in fact love the girl, and that the final 'You know how I get when I worry' sounds a note of gratuitous self-pity. In this dialogue one of the characters is lying, but it is up to the reader to detect which one.

So the writer has to choose between dialogue that conveys a complex argument directly and dialogue that is dramatically accurate. Both English and American contemporary writers are subject to strong traditions which value accuracy over intellectual complexity. In America a vein of narrative technique which runs from Mark Twain's *Huckleberry Finn* to J. D. Salinger's *Catcher In The Rye* exactly echoes the vocabulary and cadence of actual speech. In England playwrights like Harold Pinter and N. F. Simpson have shown the possibilities of modern spoken English as a dramatic medium.

But accuracy for its own sake does not produce fine dialogue: there are many dull television plays whose scripts could have been taped on the streets. We expect characters to speak authentically, but we also expect their language, however oblique or faltering, to convey things about them which they could not phrase for themselves. In other words, we ask the writer to use dialogue as a medium, and not as an end in itself.

## TWO MEAL SCENES
from *Goodbye, Columbus* by Philip Roth

*Neil Klugman the narrator is a young librarian from a poor Jewish family. He lives with his aunt in the backstreets of the New York suburb of Newark, but has fallen in love with Brenda Patimkin, a college girl from an affluent middle-class Jewish family. In the first scene Neil eats in his aunt's house; in the second he goes out to dinner with the Patimkins. In the novel the two occasions are separated by eleven pages.*

## DINNER WITH AUNT GLADYS

My aunt called me and I steeled myself for dinner.

She pushed the black whirring fan up to *High* and that way it managed to stir the cord that hung from the kitchen light.

'What kind of soda you want? I got ginger ale, plain seltzer, black raspberry, and a bottle cream soda I could open up.'

'None, thank you.'

'You want water?'

'I don't drink with my meals. Aunt Gladys, I've told you that every day for a year already—'

'Max could drink a whole case with his chopped liver only. He works hard all day. If you worked hard you'd drink more.'

At the stove she heaped up a plate with pot roast, gravy, boiled potatoes, and peas and carrots. She put it in front of me and I could feel the heat of the food in my face. Then she cut two pieces of rye bread and put that next to me, on the table.

I forked a potato in half and ate it, while Aunt Gladys, who had seated herself across from me, watched. 'You don't want bread,' she said, 'I wouldn't cut it it should go stale.'

'I *want* bread,' I said.

'You don't like with seeds, do you?'

I tore a piece of bread in half and ate it.

'How's the meat?' she said.

'Okay. Good.'

'You'll fill yourself with potatoes and bread, the meat you'll leave over I'll have to throw it out.'

Suddenly she leaped up from the chair. 'Salt!' When she returned to the table she plunked a salt shaker down in front of me—pepper wasn't served in her home: she'd heard on Galen Drake that it was not absorbed by the body, and it was disturbing to Aunt Gladys to think that anything she served might pass through a gullet, stomach, and bowel just for the pleasure of the trip.

'You're going to pick the peas out is all? You tell me that, I wouldn't buy with the carrots.'

'I love carrots,' I said, 'I love them.' And to prove it, I dumped half of them down my throat and the other half on to my trousers.

'Pig,' she said.


## DINNER WITH THE PATIMKINS

There was not much dinner conversation; eating was heavy and methodical and serious, and it would be just as well to record all that was said in one swoop, rather than indicate the sentences lost in the passing of food, the words gurgled into mouthfuls, the syntax chopped and forgotten in heapings, spillings, and gorgings.

To Ron: When's Harriet calling?

Ron: Five o'clock.

Julie: It *was* five o'clock.

Ron: Their time.

Julie: Why is it that it's earlier in Milwaukee? Suppose you took a plane back and forth all day. You'd never get older.

Brenda: That's right, sweetheart.

Mrs. P.: What do you give the child misinformation for? Is that why she goes to school?

Brenda: I don't know why she goes to school.

Mr. P. (*lovingly*): College girl.

Ron: Where's Carlota? Carlota!

Mrs. P.: Carlota, give Ronald more.

Carlota (*calling*): More what?

Ron: Everything.

Mr. P.: Me too.

Mrs. P.: They'll have to *roll* you on the links.

Mr. P. (*pulling his shirt up and slapping his black, curved belly*): What are you talking about? Look at that?

Ron (*yanking his T-shirt up*): Look at *this*.

Brenda (*to me*): Would you care to bare your middle?

Me (*the choir boy again*): No.

Mrs. P.: That's right, Neil.

Me: Yes. Thank you.

Carlota (*over my shoulder, like an unsummoned spirit*): Would *you* like more?

Me: No.

Mr. P.: He eats like a bird.

Julie: Certain birds eat a lot.

Brenda: Which ones?

Mrs. P.: Let's not talk about animals at the dinner table. Brenda, why do you encourage her?

Ron: Where's Carlota, I gotta play tonight.

Mr. P.: Tape your wrist, don't forget.

Mrs. P.: Where do you live, Bill?

Brenda: Neil.

Mrs. P.: Didn't I say Neil?

Julie: You said 'Where do you live, *Bill*?'

Mrs. P.: I must have been thinking of something else.

Ron: I hate tape. How the hell can I play in tape?

Julie: Don't curse.

Mrs. P.: That's right.

Mr. P.: What is Mantle batting now?

Julie: Three twenty-eight.

Ron: Three twenty-five.

Julie: Eight!

Ron: Five, jerk! He got three for four in the second game.

Julie: *Four* for four.

Ron: That was an error, Minoso should have had it.

Julie: *I* didn't think so.

Brenda (to me): See?

Mrs. P.: See what?

Brenda: I was talking to Bill.

Julie: Neil.

Mr. P.: Shut up and eat.

Mrs. P.: A little less talking, young lady.

Julie: *I* didn't say anything.

Brenda: She was talking to me, sweetie.

Mr. P.: What's this *she* business? Is that how you call your mother? What's dessert?

The phone rings, and though we are awaiting dessert, the meal seems at a formal end, for Ron breaks for his room, Julie shouts 'Harriet!' and Mr. Patimkin is not wholly successful in stifling a belch, though the failure even more than the effort ingratiates him to me. Mrs. Patimkin is directing Carlota not to mix the milk silverware and the meat silverware again, and Carlota is eating a peach while she listens; under the table I feel Brenda's fingers tease my calf. I am full.

ANALYSIS

There are three main voices at work here: that of the narrator, Neil Klugman, that of Aunt Gladys and that of the chorus of Patimkins. We are given distinctive speech patterns for an educated New Yorker, a poor Jewish immigrant and a family of affluent suburbanites. On a merely technical level, Roth proves an exact recorder. Neil's quizzical mixture of formal and colloquial phrasing, Aunt Gladys's twisted Yiddish-English ('You'll fill yourself with potatoes and bread, the meat you'll leave over I'll have to throw it out') and the bright facetiousness of the Patimkins, are sharply rendered. But it is in the balancing of the dialogues that the real work of the novelist has been done.

Consider the rôle of Neil Klugman in both conversations. He does not say much, and when he speaks as the narrator he is alert but non-committal. Roth concentrates on Aunt Gladys and the Patimkins, allowing Neil to drift almost without comment between the two settings. Each grouping bears close resemblance to the other; people sitting down to a meal can be expected to talk and behave in a similar fashion, and Roth draws upon the established conventions of table manners. So that when the scenes do differ, we can infer that an important statement is being made about the two ways of life exemplified by Aunt Gladys and the Patimkin family.

At the first meal, Aunt Gladys talks about nothing but food and household economies. At the second, food is hardly mentioned at all, and the conversation consists of family wise cracks, sports talk and an occasional flippant intimacy between Neil and Brenda. We can immediately locate the two groups socially: one household where money is short and good food important, the other where both are taken for granted. By education and inclination, Neil hovers somewhere between the two classes: he is embarrassed both by Aunt Gladys's perpetual fussing and by the Patimkins' brashness.

But does Roth lead us towards an evaluative judgement of

the groups or do we, as in the Hemingway dialogue, have to infer everything? Look at the structure of the dialogues, at the detailed narrative of the first and the bare script of the second. When Neil eats with Aunt Gladys, there is a warmth of description and documentation. His aunt is a strongly felt physical presence, complete with familiar prejudices and mannerisms. We feel that Neil *knows* her in a way that he cannot possibly know the Patimkins. When she exclaims '*Salt!*', Neil is able to explain 'pepper wasn't served in her home: she'd heard on Galen Drake that it was not absorbed by the body . . .' Even when Neil appears to resent Aunt Gladys, his complaints are tempered by irony, as when he announces 'I *steeled* myself for dinner'. We feel throughout the scene that both people have arrived at an intimate acceptance of one another.

In the second episode, the script form prevents Neil from making any interpretative comments. The banality of the conversation has to stand on its own, and we are immersed among a family of strangers making jokes that we don't altogether understand. No one bothers to make Neil feel at home: all the Patimkins sound complacently wrapped up in themselves. Roth further emphasizes the alien quality of their world by refusing to supply us with explanatory detail. Finally the choice between Aunt Gladys and the Patimkin family is ours, but Roth has subtly forced our hand.

# 7  Character and Manners

When an anthropologist talks of Culture he endows the word with a much larger and more inclusive meaning than it usually possesses in ordinary speech. '"A culture" refers to the distinctive way of life of a group of people, their complete "design for living"', remarks Clyde Kluckholm in an article called 'The Study of Culture'. The definition is a useful one for the literary critic, since it covers the more ambiguous literary concept of Manners. In discussing the use of manners in fiction I should like to include as relevant every distinctive feature, however trivial or transient, of the particular society portrayed in the novel.

Jean-Luc Godard the French film director has written of his 'passion for analysing what is called modern living, for dissecting it like a biologist to see what goes on underneath'. Underneath what? Godard goes on to explain his fascination with advertisements, newspapers, television, the impedimenta of city life: 'I want to cover everything—sport, politics, even groceries.' In that 'even groceries' Godard reveals the minute concern for manners which characterizes his own films and has always been a staple feature of the technique of fiction. The cultural style of a society is expressed in the most ephemeral of its products. For we are creatures of culture, subject to the local and temporary manners of our society. Fashions in dress, conversation and life-style change, and the novelist benefits immensely from the rich inventiveness of a complex and fashion-conscious society.

Manners equip the novelist with a bridge, over which he passes from talking about the individual to talking about society. How a character thinks about morality may be distinctively individual, but the way he combs his hair, the newspapers he reads, the furniture he has in his house, even the technique he uses for courting his girl friend, belong to a common culture, determined by the nature of his society and its geographical, historical and political location. If a character is to assert himself as an individual he must first transcend his culture. Conversely, some characters in fiction are so 'culture-bound' that they never become individuals in their own right. We might remember Elinor Dashwood's remarks to her sister in Jane Austen's *Sense and Sensibility*, after Marianne has spent a rapturous morning quizzing the handsome Mr. Willoughby:

> 'For *one* morning I think you have done pretty well. You have already ascertained Mr. Willoughby's opinion in almost every matter of importance. You know what he thinks of Cowper and Scott; you are certain of his estimating their beauties as he ought, and you have received every assurance of his admiring Pope no more than is proper. But how is your acquaintance to be long supported under such extraordinary dispatch of every subject for discourse?'

When Marianne replies, fearing that she has been 'open and sincere where I ought to have been reserved', we are conscious of some disparity between her own assessment of her performance and the performance itself. For of course she has explored nothing of importance in Mr. Willoughby: she has merely ascertained that they both share the manners of their common society. When two people in the early nineteenth century disdained Pope and adored Cowper and Scott, they did not reveal an amazing coincidence of taste and opinion; they merely voiced the conventional prejudices of their time. (One should add that to reverse that judgement in the 1960's is to voice the conventional prejudices of our own time.) The important point here lies in the fact that characters may be most subject to their culture at just those moments when they think they have reached a pinnacle of individuality.

The existence of a body of manners enables the novelist to place his characters in a social setting, to give them a physical presence and credible existence, without telling us any more about the characters *themselves* than Marianne knows of Mr. Willoughby. When Henry James begins *The Europeans* he sketches the refinement of a sophisticated man and woman staying at the best hotel in Boston. It is important that at this stage we see nothing more of the characters than the fashionable decorum of their social milieu. For the moment James does not even attach names to the two people: they are generalized figures representative of a class and a culture. Here James introduces the lady, whom we know later as Eugenia, Baroness Munster:

> The lady brushed past him in her walk; her much-trimmed skirts were voluminous. She never dropped her eyes upon his work; she only turned them, occasionally, as she passed, to a mirror suspended above a toilet-table on the other side of the room. Here she paused a moment, gave a pinch to her waist with her two hands, or raised these members—they were very plump and pretty—to the multifold braids of her hair, with a movement half-caressing, half-corrective.

This portrait of a woman of leisure in the mid-nineteenth century is established solely on details of fashion: the ample layered skirts, the waist pinched by whalebone stays, the braided hair, of the time. Even Eugenia's physique is controlled by the manners of the period. James says of her hands that they were 'plump and pretty'. Victorian taste favoured pale, pudgy hands in which the knuckles were invisible, each covered by a dimple of flesh. Eugenia's fashion-plate existence is perfectly suited to James's purpose. Through her and her brother we are initiated into the cosmopolitan culture of the 1870s: she is a living embodiment of that culture, its ideal of beauty, its clothes, its language, its class assumptions.

When contemporary English novelists exploit the manners of

our own time, they turn most characteristically towards small-scale institutions with their professional rituals and codes of conduct. Kingsley Amis's *Lucky Jim* and Malcolm Bradbury's *Eating People Is Wrong* discover a rich comic texture in the life of a red-brick university with its faculty politics and intellectual pretensions. Roy Fuller's *Image of a Society* is a study of a building society and the manners of office work. John Bowen sets his *Storyboard* in an advertising agency, saturating it with details of the jargon, dress and attitudes of copywriters and account executives. In *The Garrick Year*, Margaret Drabble paints an acid portrait of a theatre company in which the actors' tribal behaviour dominates the novel.

In America J. D. Salinger chronicles the manners of teenagers, college students and the young affluent middle classes. His novels, *Catcher In The Rye*, *Franny and Zooey*, *Raise High The Roofbeams*, *Carpenter*, and *Seymour, An Introduction*, work as exact registers of their time, catching speech mannerisms, reading habits and gestures with studied accuracy. He recreates in his work the intensely observed surface of modern campus and apartment life.

Perhaps the most assiduous and effective living analyst of manners is Mary McCarthy. Her sharp, deflationary portraits of vaguely highbrow, mildly radical intellectuals and professionals are rich in humour and penetrating in their insights. *The Group*, from which the example for this chapter was taken, is a brilliant piece of surgery: Miss McCarthy has opened a section of contemporary culture with clinical precision.

## PORTRAIT OF LIBBY MacAUSLAND
from *The Group* by Mary McCarthy

The Group *is a study of eight women who graduated from Vassar College in 1933. In this extract we are introduced to Libby MacAusland shortly after her graduation as she attempts to establish herself as a woman of letters in New York.*

Libby MacAusland had a spiffy apartment in the Village. Her family in Pittsfield was helping her pay the rent. The job she had been promised by a publisher, just before graduation, had not exactly materialized. The man she had interviewed, who was one of the partners in the firm, had shown her around the offices, given her some books they published, and introduced her to an editor, who was smoking a pipe in his sanctum. Mr. LeRoy, a portly young man with a dark moustache and bushy eyebrows, had been very forthcoming as long as the partner was there, but afterwards, instead of settling her at a desk right away (Libby had spied an empty cubby-hole in the editorial department), he had told her to come back in a week or so. Then he said he was going to give her manuscripts to read at home to try her out. They paid $5 apiece for reading a manuscript and writing a summary and an opinion, and she ought to be able, he thought, to do three a week, which was the same as having a half-time job—better. 'If we started you in the office,' he said, 'we could only give you $25 full time. And you'd have your car fare and your lunches to pay.' When he asked her if she needed the work, Libby had let on that she did; she thought if he thought she was pretty desperate he would find her more manuscripts to read.

Anyway, that ought not to have been his business. Her background was perfect for a berth in publishing: fluent reading knowledge of French and Italian; copy editing, proof reading, and dummying as editor in chief of the Vassar literary magazine; short-story and verse-writing courses; good command of typing —all the tools of the trade. But mindful of the competition, Libby took special pains with her reports for Mr. LeRoy, typing them triple-spaced on a kind of sky-blue typing paper that was still manufactured in one of the mills in Pittsfield and stapling them in stiff blue covers. The 'presentation' of her themes had been outstanding at Vassar. She always added a title page with a colophon—her device, the same she used for her bookplate— to her weekly papers and put them between covers; her handwriting was distinctive, with Greek e's and embellished capitals. Miss Kitchel had noticed her immediately in English 105 as 'the artistic young lady with the fine Italian hand'. Her 'effusions', as Miss Kitchel, who was a hearty soul, used to call them, had been printed in the freshman *Sampler*, and she had been invited, while still a freshman, to serve on the board of the literary magazine. Libby's forte was descriptive writing. 'This hopeful beauty did create' (Carew) was the motto beneath her picture in the year-book.

Her mother's sister had a villa in Fiesole, and Libby had spent a year there as a child, going to the sweetest dame school in Florence, and countless summers afterwards—to be exact, two; Libby was prone to exaggerate. She spoke a breathless Italian, with a nifty Tuscan accent, and had been dying to take her junior year abroad, at the University of Bologna, for she had read a fascinating novel called *The Lady of Laws*, about a learned lady in Renaissance times who had been a doctor of law at Bologna had got raped and carried off by one of the Malatestas (Libby had been an alternate in a debate on censorship with Wesleyan freshman year). But she had misdoubted that being a year away from college might cost her the 'crown' she coveted; she counted on being elected President of Students.

Libby played basketball (centre) and had a big following among the dimmer bulbs of the class; she was president of the Circolo Italiano and had been president of the class sophomore year. She was also active in the Community Church. But running for President of Students, she had been mowed down, as it turned out, by the big guns of the North Tower group, who were more the hockey-playing, ground-gripper, rah-rah Vassar sort and carried off all the class offices senior year. They had asked her to group with them at the end of freshman year, but she had thought Lakey's crowd was snazzier. Came the dawn when Lakey and the others would not even electioneer for her.

It seemed to be Libby's fate (so far) to start out strong with people and then have them lose interest for no reason she could see—'They flee from me that some time did me seek.' That had happened with the group. Libby adored *Of Human Bondage* and Katherine Mansfield and Edna Millay and Elinor Wylie and quite a lot of Virginia Woolf, but she could never get anybody to talk with her about books any more, because Lakey said her taste was sentimental. The paradox was that she was the most popular member of the group *outside* and the least popular *inside*. For instance, she had put Helena, who was one to hide her light under a bushel, on the board of the literary magazine; then Helena had blandly turned around and sided with a minority that wanted to print 'experimental literature'. She and the arch-enemy, Norine Schmittlapp, had collaborated on an 'Open Letter to the Editor', claiming that the college magazine no longer represented Vassar writing but had become the inheritance of a 'pallid' literary clique. Libby, counselled by the faculty, had let herself run with the current and printed an 'experimental number'; the tide turned *her* way when one of the poems in it proved to be a hoax, written by a cute freshman as a spoof on modern poetry. But in the very next issue a story she had battled for was discovered to be plagiarized, word for word, from a story in *Harper's*. It was hushed up, for the sake of the girl's future, after the Dean had had a talk with *Harper's* about it, but someone (probably Kay) whom Libby had told in strictest confidence betrayed her, and soon the rebel clique was busy spreading the news. It was one thing, they said, to be generously taken in by a hoax and another to print as original writing an unadventurous theft from a stale, second-rate magazine. Libby literally could not understand this last part; one of her highest ambitions was to have a story or a poem published by *Harper's*. And lo and behold, hold your hats, girls, it had happened to her finally a year ago this last winter.

She had been in New York nearly two years now, living first with two other girls from Pittsfield in Tudor City and now alone, in this spiffy apartment she had found. She was avid for success, and her parents were willing; Brother was settled, at long last, in a job in the mill, and Sister had married a Harkness. So Libby was free to try her pinions.

Mr. LeRoy had given her stacks of manuscripts to start out with. She had had to buy a lady's briefcase at Mark Cross to lug them all back and forth—black calf, very snazzy. 'You're *made*, Libby!' her room-mates in Tudor City used to gasp when they saw her stagger in with her load. And to pile Pelion on Ossa, she had got herself some book-review assignments from the *Saturday Review of Literature* and the *Herald Tribune Books*—no less. Her room-mates were green with envy because they were only going to Katherine Gibbs Secretarial School themselves. Her family was jubilant; that was why they had let her have the apartment. Libby was obviously dedicated to the idea of a literary career, as Brother reported to headquarters when he came home from a visit to New York. Father had had her first cheque photostatted and framed for her, and it hung above her desk, with a little branch of laurel from the parental garden, to show that she was crowned with bays.

ANALYSIS

Libby is cast almost entirely within the mould of her culture. She is a stereotype; expensively educated, romantically committed to the sidelines of literature, conventionally ambitious and anxious to conform to the standards of her milieu. The whole passage is soaked in the manners of the Vassar 'Class of 33'; Libby represents one facet of their common identity and style. She is the 'literary' member of the group, but even in her personal specialism she expresses group values and group taste.

Underlying this portrait—as it underlies the whole novel—is

an essentially economic classification of the group members. A Vassar education is a luxury few can afford, and the power of money animates the occupations and attitudes of all the girls. Libby's parents, we note, help her to pay the rent of her 'spiffy apartment' in Greenwich Village (a select, and self-consciously bohemian quarter of New York). Her aunt owns an Italian villa and Libby herself is accustomed to vacations in Europe—so accustomed to them, in fact, that she can afford to miss her 'Junior Year Abroad' in order to run for the office of Student President. Her typing paper, her briefcase, her readiness to be subsidized in her career by her parents, allocate her to a financially privileged class. That curious ritual of the photostatted cheque crowned by laurel bays is a neat touch: success and money are inextricably wedded, but we feel, nevertheless, that Libby is free of financial necessity: money is primarily only a symbol to her.

On a rather more specific level, Miss McCarthy locates Libby in a very closely defined social area. Her parents, brother and sister occupy an important place in the narrative; clearly Libby is part of a tight-knit family group, centred on the parental 'headquarters' from which the businessman father directs operations. Furthermore, Libby 'was . . . active in the Community Church', and involved in the team games and internal politics of the university. She is remarkable in her conformity to the norms of the manufacturing upper-middle class: loyal to her parents and their values, adherent to the mores of her college, ready to adopt the new code of the publisher's office, Libby is a model of social adjustment and a perfect product of her class.

Perhaps one expects her to deviate most in her literary taste, but even here she proves a dedicated follower of convention. She manages to incorporate among the books she 'adores' examples of every height and depth of brow: '*Of Human Bondage* and Katherine Mansfield and Edna Millay and Elinor Wylie and quite a lot of Virginia Woolf.' Her reading appears to be far-ranging and indiscriminate: the qualification of 'quite a lot of' Virginia Woolf is the most significant clue that Libby lets fall—even the boundaries of her sensibility are commonplace ones. Yet Miss McCarthy wields a double-edged blade when she deals with the *Harper's* affair. For Libby, as a prototypical middle-brow, easily accepts the glamour of this conventionally sophisticated magazine while the rest of her class mates affect to scorn it. Whether their scorn, or Libby's ingenuous reverence, is most at fault in Miss McCarthy's eyes is a matter of some ambiguity. Obviously, though, the standing of the *Saturday Review of Literature* and the *Herald Tribune Books* is beyond question.

The whole tone of the narration echoes the student idiom of the group. Helena Davidson, another member, writes the class notes for the *Alumnae Magazine* and her flippantly smart style provides Miss McCarthy with a basic key for the novel. She strikes a consistent note of nineteen-thirties *chic*, using the slang and syntax of fashionable gossip-columns of the period with their racy, if now faded, elegance. 'Spiffy', 'nifty' and 'snazzy' are favourite adjectives, indiscriminately applied: Libby has 'a nifty Tuscan accent'. Figures of speech have a facetious pedantry about them: 'the dimmer bulbs of the class . . . lo and behold, hold your hats, girls . . . to pile Pelion on Ossa . . . Brother reported to headquarters . . .' Many of the constructions are mannered and self-conscious: 'Came the dawn when . . . start out strong with people . . . countless summers afterwards . . .' The total effect of the language of the passage is to evoke a sense of strained informality and hearty with-itness. Everything that happens has to be contained, however awkwardly, within the jargon of the group. Language in this case is a form of private code; it enables group members to share their experiences by means of an arbitrary set of personal symbols. The special adjectives and phrases are an integral part of the group's system of manners; they set the trademark of fashionability on whatever they describe.

John Gross began his *New Statesman* review on *The Group* with, 'In her new novel Mary McCarthy sets out to humiliate a group of girls who graduated from Vassar in 1933.' There is much justice in his comment, and it raises important questions about the use of manners to portray character. Before she can bring her armoury of reading lists, class rituals, eating habits and language into play, Miss McCarthy has to credit the reader with a degree of superior knowingness. You, she seems to say, will see how trivial or pretentious these attitudes are. Since her readership must be largely composed of the kind of people who inhabit her books, she involves herself in a paradox, flattering our intellectual snobbery on the one hand, and attacking it on the other. She makes accomplices of us all, inviting us to watch her characters make fools of themselves from a height of unearned and vicarious sophistication. At the same time one is forced to admit that a major aspect of modern culture has been catalogued with deadly accuracy. As a novelist of manners, Miss McCarthy manages to touch the pulse of the dominant social class of her time, but she often raises a secondary question: can she be accused of cheating in her performance?

# 8 Character and Symbolism

Just as dialogue and manners can be used by the novelist to 'place' his characters socially and culturally, so a fabric of symbolism may enable the writer to create a moral and intellectual framework for the action of his novel. Symbolism allows an author to link the limited world of his characters to one of the great systems of values, so that we are made to compare the happenings in the novel with their mythological or historical parallels. Specific actions in the story illustrate general patterns of behaviour, and the private character acquires a new importance when he is seen in the light of his symbolic counterpart.

A system of symbolism usually depends on the existence of a commonly known body of ideas or beliefs. In western literature three basic systems recur most frequently; the symbolism of Christianity, of classical mythology and of Romanticism. One of these three sources illuminates almost every major symbolic novel in our language.

Christian morality is of course ingrained into the history of the novel. But it is not until fairly recently that novelists have gone to the Bible as a source of myth, creating characters who are closely identifiable with biblical figures and events. The hero of William Faulkner's *Light In August* is called Joe Christmas, echoing the initials and name of Jesus Christ himself. Joe is an orphan, and as a 'white-negro' is despised or feared by both whites and negroes in the southern state in which he lives. An outcast, he drifts from job to job, anxious to love but denied the chance to express it. Faulkner traces his suffering at the hands of his fellows until the climax of the book, when Christmas is shot dead in a minister's house by an hysterical fascist. *Light In August* gains a great deal from the depth of its symbolic parallels: Faulkner invites us to view his hero as a frustrated and persecuted Christ-figure, crucified by the violence and prejudice of a world he cannot escape. Recent fiction provides many comparable examples of the quarrying of Christian myth. Dougal Douglas in *The Ballad of Peckham Rye* is Muriel Spark's contemporary Satan, witty, engaging and amoral. And in William Golding's *Free Fall* the painter Sammy Mountjoy re-enacts the fall of Adam in his search for knowledge. Significantly, both Miss Spark and Mr. Golding are professed Christians. For the use of a Christian symbolic framework tends to involve an implicit moral statement. Where Christian symbolism is inherently 'ethically committed', symbolism derived from classical mythology or Romanticism is 'ethically neutral': when a writer employs either of these two latter systems he does not necessarily indicate a direct moral evaluation of the behaviour of his characters.

Beneath James Joyce's *Ulysses* runs the sub-text of Homer's *Odyssey*. As Leopold Bloom is followed around Dublin during his nine hundred and thirty page long day, he is shadowed by the ghost of that earlier Ulysses. The classical parallel provides a continuing commentary on Bloom as he wanders about Dublin meeting modern versions of the Sirens, of Nestor, of the Cyclops, of Nausicaa. Less satisfactory is John Updike's use of classical symbolism in *The Centaur*. This novel is worth glancing at, if for no other reason than that it demonstrates how impossibly far a symbolic technique is sometimes taken. Updike's novel is all ingenuity and subtle parallels: it demands, not so much to be read as to be decoded. From the moment that his schoolmaster-hero is wounded in the foot with an arrow Updike sets us on a long and arduous trail of classical allusion. One possible reason for the comparative dearth of classical symbolism in the modern novel is the fact that few readers are adequately equipped to follow such a sustained course of reference to Latin and Greek mythology.

Romanticism replaces the system of mythological characters with a system of Nature, and people are defined against a natural world which is pregnant with meaning. Sun, moon and wilderness make a living commentary on the lives of the human beings in the novel, so that we see the characters set in the universal frame of Nature. Think, for instance, of Emily Brontë's *Wuthering Heights*. The bleak moors around the Heights are a constant reminder of the chaos that threatens to destroy the household. Heathcliff, whose name is itself a compound of moorland qualities, can be seen as the living embodiment of that chaos, an agent of indifferent destruction. Throughout the novel he is associated with ferocity, inscrutability and, on at least one occasion, with 'Nature'. All the other characters in the novel are defined by their relationship to him. At one extreme the Lintons, to whom he is completely alien, are sickly and over-civilized; at the other Cathy, who loves him, recognizes in him that mysterious quality of force which to some extent she shares herself. Heathcliff has many parallels in fiction. In Melville's *Moby Dick* the white whale similarly embodies the indifference of Nature. It is deceptively beautiful, incomprehensible and devastatingly powerful. Moby Dick exercises a total fascination over Captain Ahab, and through him the whale controls the fate of all the other characters in the novel. Beside such power people are puny things: Melville's symbolism of Nature puts them in a belittling perspective.

These then are the three main sources from which the novelist may make a symbolic commentary on his characters. But the contemporary writer occupies rather a special position; he is likely to be at least vaguely familiar with the assumptions of psychoanalysis which have considerably influenced our ideas of the importance of symbolism. Carl Jung formulated a concept of 'archetypal myth' in which he maintained that certain basic images, of birth, growth, rebirth, infinitude, represented by natural objects and figures, were historically implanted in the mind of man. The circle, the life-cycle of the plant, the movement of the sea, reflect, in Jungian terms, unconscious human urges. Correspondingly, the great mythological stories could be explained as expressions of a collective, supra-rational impulse. The resurrection, for instance, could be identified with pagan rebirth myths and Christian ritual could be seen to bear close resemblance to fertility rites which long pre-date Christianity itself. Jung's work reinvigorated the possibilities of symbolism just at the time when it seemed that no ethical system could claim absolute value. It suggested that all patterns of belief are related to some interdependent primal need. For the novelist this meant that the action of his book, whatever its nominal mythology, could draw on a spring of feeling which runs deeper than explanation or avowed belief. One might add a rider to this theory, indicating that some novelists have taken it to mean that they should create patterns of symbolism as wilfully inscrutable as Moby Dick himself. They are, mercifully, in a minority however.

### THE ROSE GARDEN EPISODE
from *The Sandcastle* by Iris Murdoch

*Mor, a housemaster at a minor public school, and his wife Nan, have been to dinner with Demoyte, a retired headmaster. Rain Carter, a painter staying with Demoyte, has been commissioned by the school to do a portrait of him. The episode begins as Nan and Mor prepare to leave for home.*

'I think we ought to be starting for home,' said Nan, after some little time. She looked at Mor.

'Yes, I suppose so,' said Mor. He did not want to go yet.

Nan rose with determination. Demoyte did not try to detain

her. The company began to drift in a polite group towards the door.

'I asked Handy to cut you some roses,' said Demoyte, 'but I have an uneasy feeling she's forgotten. Handy!' He shouted over the bannisters, 'Roses for Mrs. Mor!'

Mor was touched. He knew that the roses were really for him, in response to his having, a few days ago, expressed admiration for the rose garden.

Miss Handforth appeared from the kitchen with a loud clack of the green baize door. 'I didn't get down the garden today,' she announced.

'Well, get down *now*.' said Demoyte in an irritated tone. He was tired of the evening.

'You know I can't see in the dark,' said Miss Handforth, well aware that Demoyte was not serious. 'Besides, the dew is down.'

Nan said simultaneously, 'Don't bother, please. They would have been *lovely*, but now don't bother.' Mor knew that she was not interested in the roses. Nan thought on the whole that flowers were rather messy and insanitary things. But she was quite pleased all the same to be able to underline that Handy was in the wrong.

'Let me go!' said Miss Carter suddenly. 'I can see in the dark. I know where the roses are. Let me cut some for Mrs. Mor.' She ran ahead of them down the wide staircase.

'Capital!' said Demoyte. 'Handy, give her the big scissors from the hall drawer. You go with her, Mor, and see she really knows the way. I'll entertain your lady. But for Christ's sake don't be long.'

Miss Carter took the scissors and vanished through the front door. Mor ran after her, and closed the door behind him. The night was cool and very dark. He could not see, but knew the way without sight to the wooden door in the wall that led into the main garden. He heard the door clap before him, and in a moment he felt its surface under his hand, cool and yielding.

He emerged on to the quiet dewy lawn. He heard the distant traffic and saw the interrupted flashes from the headlights, but all about him was dark and still. He blinked, and saw ahead of him the small figure hurrying away across the lawn.

'Miss Carter!' said Mor in a low voice, 'wait for me, I'm coming too.' After the brilliance of the house the garden was strange, pregnant with trees and bushes, open to the dew and the stars. He felt almost alarmed.

Miss Carter had stopped and was waiting for him. She seemed less tiny now that there were no objects with which to compare her. He saw her eyes glint in the darkness. 'This way,' she said.

Mor blundered after her. 'Yes, you can see in the dark,' he said. 'I wish I could.' They went through the yew hedge under the archway into the second garden.

They walked quietly across the lawn. Mor felt strangely breathless. Miss Carter was laying her feet very softly to the earth and made no sound at all as she walked. Mor tried to step softly too, but he could feel and hear under his feet the moisture in the close-cropped grass. An intense perfume of damp earth and darkened flowers surrounded them and quenched the noises of the world outside. Mor could see very little, but he continued to follow the dark moving shape of the girl ahead. He was still dazed by the swiftness of the transition.

They reached the steps which led up into the third garden. Miss Carter went up the steps like a bird and for a moment he saw the pallor of her bare arm exposed against the black holly bush as she turned to wait for him. Mor plunged forward, his foot seeking the lowest step. He stumbled and almost fell.

'Here, come this way,' she said from above him, 'this way.' She kept her voice soft, compelled to by the garden. Then she came back down the steps and he realized that she was reaching out her hand. Mor took her hand in his and let her guide him up the steps. Her grip was firm. They passed between the black holly bushes, and released each other. Mor felt a strong shock within him, as if very distantly something had subsided or given way. He had a confused feeling of surprise. The moon came out of the clouds for a moment and suddenly the sky was seen in motion.

The rose garden was about them now, narrowing towards the place where Demoyte's estate ended in the avenue of mulberry trees. Mor had never seen it by night. It looked different now, as if the avenue were immensely long, and Mor had a strange momentary illusion that it was in that direction that the house lay, far off at the end of the avenue: Demoyte's house, or else its double, where everything happened with a difference.

'*Quelle merveille!*' said Miss Carter in a low voice. She took a few quick steps across the grass, and then stopped, lifting her face to the moonlight. A moment later she began to run and threw her arms about the trunk of the first mulberry tree of the avenue. The branches above her were murmuring like a river.

Mor coughed. He was slightly embarrassed by these transports. 'You know, we musn't be too long,' he said.

'Yes, yes,' said Miss Carter, detaching herself from the tree, 'we shall pick them very quickly now.' She began to run between the beds, picking out the buds which were just partly open. The scissors snicked and the long-stemmed roses were cast on to the grass. The moon whitened the paler ones and made the dark ones more dark, like blood. Mor tried to pick a rose, but as he had nothing with which to cut it he only pricked himself and mangled the rose.

'Leave all to me,' said Miss Carter, coming to snip off the dangling blossom. 'There, that should be enough.'

Mor was anxious to get back now. He had a vision of Nan and Demoyte waiting impatiently in the hall. Also, there was something which he wanted to think over. He hastened ahead down the stone steps, his eyes now accustomed to the dark, and ran noisily across the lawn to the yew hedge. Here he waited, and held the iron gate open for Miss Carter. It clinked to behind them, and now they could see the lighted windows of the house where already Miss Handforth had drawn back the curtains in preparation for the night. They passed the wooden gate, and in a moment they were blinking and rubbing their eyes in the bright light of the hall. Miss Carter clutched the great armful of roses to her breast.

'What an age you were,' said Nan. 'Did you get lost?'

'No,' said Mor, 'it was just very dark.'

'Here are the roses,' said Miss Carter, trying to detach them from where they had pinned themselves to her cotton blouse. 'What about some paper to put them in?'

'Here, have the *Evening News*,' said Demoyte, taking it from the table. 'I haven't read it, but to the devil with it, now the day is over.'

ANALYSIS

The centre of interest in this extract is not in the characters themselves so much as in the rose garden and its enveloping darkness. Everybody in the episode acts according to their particular relationship to the roses. The first few paragraphs establish us solidly in a polite, mundane world. As the guests file out after the dinner party, Miss Murdoch catches their conventionality, their effusiveness, their essential dullness. Miss Handforth cannot see in the dark; Nan thinks roses are 'rather messy and insanitary things'; Demoyte is 'not serious' when he orders his housekeeper into the garden. As long as Miss Murdoch keeps us inside the house, the atmosphere is stuffy and decorous. Only one character stands out: when Rain Carter says 'I can see in the dark', she sets herself apart from all the other characters. As a painter, she has a depth of vision, in both a literal and a figurative sense, denied to the others.

The narrative point of view is largely Mor's, and he quite clearly is used to living in the polite, non-visionary world of the house. But at the same time he is not blindly dogmatic like Nan or Miss Handforth. When he goes into the garden with Rain he is a willing, if inept, pupil, ready to be shown whatever mystery the roses have to offer. The consistency of the passage comes largely from the repeated contrasts between Mor and Rain.

Mor cannot see in the dark; he moves clumsily, stumbling and noisy; when he tries to pick a rose, he only pricks himself and mangles the flower. Rain the visionary moves 'like a bird', making 'no sound at all as she walked.' She picks roses with speed and absolute precision. The dark garden seems her natural habitat and she acquires a freedom there which is wholly alien to the rigorous social conventions of the house.

> A moment later she began to run and threw her arms about the trunk of the first mulberry tree of the avenue. The branches above her were murmuring like a river. Mor coughed. He was slightly embarrassed by these transports.

Mor has a foot in both camps. He has the capacity to wonder at the strangeness and beauty of the garden, but he is not at ease there. It is with relief that he lets the garden gate close behind him and goes back into the house, to Nan's prosaic question and Demoyte's unread *Evening News*.

In the context of the whole novel, and in the force of the incident itself, the episode in the rose garden is an important turning point in Mor's development as a character. A sketchy reading of the passage probably makes us aware that the house represents limiting social conventions, while the garden embodies a deeper, freer life of mystery and imagination. But close analysis reveals a remarkable texture of symbolic implications, all of which are relevant to a full reading of the novel.

The rose garden as a place of enchantment, has many literary precedents, the most striking of which is, perhaps, Lewis

Carroll's *Alice In Wonderland*. Mor himself is not unlike Alice in his bemused anxiety to behave properly in a completely foreign world. And in the paragraph where Demoyte's house seems to be reflected at the far end of the avenue, there is an echo of the mirror image that is the basis of *Through The Looking Glass*.

The plants and colours that are named in the episode all have ancient symbolic connotations. In medieval and romantic literature the rose is associated with beauty, transience and fertility. The yew is the graveyard tree, suggesting death and infinitude. The holly and the mulberry are both symbols of fertility; the holly is the plant that stays green through the winter, the mulberry is the first spring bush to bloom. The recurrent colours are the red and white of the roses and the black of night. It is appropriate that the moon should appear from behind the clouds when Mor undergoes the shock of initiation (just as the moon dominates the climax points of Coleridge's 'The Ancient Mariner'). The moon, goddess of the imagination, presides over the enchanted garden.

Throughout the passage there are repeated images of movement: Rain herself, as she runs through the garden, is a mercurial figure. When the moon comes out from the clouds, 'the sky was seen in motion'. When Rain embraces the mulberry tree, 'the branches above her were murmuring like a river'. Associated with the intensified life of the garden is a sense of energetic freedom, and it is implicitly contrasted with the stiff formalities of Demoyte's house.

But where all these elements tend to produce a stylized tapestry of symbolism, the presence of Mor throws the symbolic texture of the passage into relief. For Mor, like Alice, is a stranger to the garden and all it represents. He is very much a contemporary figure, uncertain of himself and of his values. His readiness to be led by Rain, his embarrassment and his eventual relief at escaping the garden, make him into that familiar figure of modern fiction, the stumbling, unheroic hero.

But the major question that this passage raises is not immediately answered. Does the weight of importance that Miss Murdoch attaches to her symbolic framework stifle her characters? Do they live as believable people, or only as pawns of the symbolism? Most important of all: how desirable is it that characters in a novel should live a life of their own, independent of the novelist's technical devices? The rose garden episode illustrates one of the fundamental problems of the contemporary writer: how far can he afford to control his characters?

# 9 Character and Location

We have already seen how the novelist may 'locate' his characters by means of dialogue, manners and symbolism. In this chapter I want to use the word 'location' with the special meaning assigned to it by the film maker. In the movies, a 'location' is usually some appropriate landscape against which the characters of the film are defined. In a recent radio talk on Westerns, Laurence Kitchin made this comment on John Ford's classic picture, *Stagecoach*:

> What are its virtues? First of all, a stunning and relevant landscape. The brooding erosion sculpture of Monument Valley is not only a gift to the camera in mass and silhouette; it represents literally the antiquity of geological time. A contrasting stage for vulnerable humans, it joins with them in a compact 'objective correlative' of the pioneer's west which needs no spelling out.

That sense of the visual interaction between character and landscape can be as striking a feature of fiction as it is a necessary element in cinema. And while the twentieth-century development of the movies has sharpened the writer's awareness of the technique, effective landscape is not essentially a modern device. On the first page of Edgar Allan Poe's famous horror story, 'The Fall of The House of Usher', we are introduced to the physical appearance of the house:

> I looked upon the scene before me—upon the mere house, and the simple landscape features of the domain—upon the bleak walls—upon the vacant eye-like windows—upon a few

rank sedges—and upon a few white trunks of decayed trees—
with an utter depression of soul . . .

With the anachronism of hindsight we could label Poe's effect
as 'cinematic', and guess with fair accuracy how Alfred Hitch-
cock would deal with those white trunks and rank sedges.
Right from the beginning of 'The Fall of The House of Usher',
the sickly landscape takes charge of the characters and they act
out their story of a family's degeneration determined by the
emotional tone of the visual setting. As people, they are entirely
overshadowed by the physical presence of their surroundings:
they have no moral qualities or choices; they are subject only to
the inevitability of decay.

On a less extreme level, Dickens makes interesting use of the
technique in *David Copperfield* when David is shown the
drowned body of Steerforth lying on the shore after the wreck of
his ship:

> He led me to the shore. And on that part of it where she
> and I had looked for shells, two children—on that part of it
> where some lighter fragments of the old boat, blown down
> last night, had been scattered by the wind—among the ruins
> of the home he had wronged—I saw him lying with his head
> upon his arm, as I had often seen him lie at school.

Landscape here is not the determining factor in the scene, but
Dickens uses it to confirm the statement he is making about
Steerforth. The ruins, the fragments of wreckage and the stillness
of the aftermath act as physical correlates to Dickens's elegy on the
dead man. But the visual quality of the passage extends beyond
imagery. Dickens anticipates the devices of the cinema when he
makes David connect the storm-strewn beach with the place
where he hunted for shells in childhood and associate the body
of Steerforth with the figure of the sleeping schoolboy. For the
logic that underlies these transitions does not belong to the

intellection of narrative. Instead it stems from the linkage of things seen: a glimpsed echo of similarity is turned into a natural bridge between past and present, between, in Dickens's terms, the tranquillity of childhood and the tragic calm of death. Curiously that paragraph from a nineteenth-century novel can be translated with no significant changes into material for a screenplay:

1. Shot of David and the fisherman walking to the beach after the storm.
*Dissolve to:*
2. David and Emily searching for shells on the same beach.
*Dissolve to:*
3. Wreckage of ship and Peggotty's house.
*Cut*
4. The body of Steerforth.
*Dissolve to:*
5. Steerforth sleeping as a boy.

The way in which this passage easily adapts itself to cinematic terms is expecially interesting in that it antedates a very common practice in modern writing. The novel of short scenes linked by visual 'dissolves' became a characteristic form during the nineteen-twenties. John Dos Passos's *U.S.A.* manipulates a large cast of characters, places and incidents by cutting from one to another, often allowing each no more than a paragraph of writing. The consistency of the novel is largely maintained by the unity of location: New York City broods throughout over its varied inhabitants. Quite clearly the treatment of character in silent films, where everything had to be sketched in visual terms, opened up a wide range of new possibilities for the novelist. He was able to imitate the effects of cinema and by-pass the lengthy descriptions and deductions of discursive narrative. He, and his audience, were being educated into *seeing* characters and their actions, as well as just thinking about them.

When the movies became talkies in 1926, Hollywood began to give jobs to an increasing army of writers. A high proportion of the American novelists of the period earned their living by producing film scripts: Theodore Dreiser, William Faulkner, Scott Fitzgerald, Nathanael West, among many others, worked for the big film companies. Inevitably, a complex relationship grew up between the writers and the cinema industry. The writers learned the techniques of film-making from the inside, and transferred their new technical skills to their fiction. In the twenty-five years following Al Jolson's historic line, 'Hear me talking to you?' in the first talking film, *The Jazz Singer*, a new fictional *genre*, the 'Hollywood Novel', was developed. Novels like *Spider Boy* by Carl Van Vechten, *The Last Tycoon* by F. Scott Fitzgerald, *The Disenchanted* and *What Makes Sammy Run?* by Budd Schulberg, and *The Deer Park* by Norman Mailer, applied some of the visual techniques of Hollywood to the subject of Hollywood itself. Probably the best Hollywood novel of all, Nathanael West's *Day of the Locust*, is a magnificent blending of subject matter and literary technique. West's novel, like *U.S.A.*, is a series of short scenes juxtaposed against one another by a complicated assembly of cuts and dissolves. The location of Hollywood, with its incredible jumble of architectural styles, its mock-Chinese pagodas set against mock-Tudor cottages, its elaborate film sets manned by armies of extras in period costumes, and its atmosphere of visual blatancy and extravagance, is used by West to validate his exploration of the pitiably artificial and pretentious lives of his characters.

Since 1939, when *Day of the Locust* was published, the appeal of Hollywood has lost some of its cutting edge. Writers are still employed by the cinema (in England, the careers of Robert Bolt, Bill Naughton and Harold Pinter testify to the capacity of the movies to attract considerable talent) but time has dulled the importance of the film world as a subject for action. Nevertheless, the techniques of the screenplay have been absorbed: a sense of location and visual logic are characteristic features of contemporary writing. For the centrepiece of this section I have chosen an extract from a novel by Penelope Mortimer, an English writer who has worked on documentary films and been a professional critic of the cinema.

## THE SCENE IN THE TOWER
### from *The Pumpkin Eater* by Penelope Mortimer

*Mrs. Jake Armitage is married, for the fourth time, to a philandering script-writer. Throughout the novel she is surrounded by her children, by a circle of glib friends, and by an overwhelming sense of her own isolation. Her marriage reaches the point of breakdown when she discovers that her husband is having an affair with an actress. The only undeniably positive action she has done is to have had a tall tower built as a wing of her country cottage. In the last chapter of the book she goes alone to the tower to reconsider and reconstruct.*

I went to the tower. There, in a cell of brick and glass, I sat and watched the wall of sky that rose ten feet away from my look-out window. Nothing else existed. Nobody else lived. A thick mist packed the surrounding valleys and rain, very fine rain, fell incessantly to obscure the world further. The birds clattered, invisible: or sometimes drifted like burnt paper across the window, were carried up and away again, lying on their wings as though half asleep.

I seemed to be alone in the world. My past, at last, was over. I had given it up; set it free; sent it back where it belonged, to fit into other people's lives. For one's past grows to a point where it is longer than one's future, and then it can become too great a burden. I had found, or had created, a neutrality between the past that I had lost and the future that I feared: an interminable hour which passed under my feet like the shadow of moving stairs, each stair recurring again and again, flattening to meet the next, a perfect circle of isolation captive between yesterday and tomorrow, between two illusions. Yesterday had never been. Tomorrow would never come. Darkness and light succeeded each other. The thick log in the grate became a heap of ash. Did this mean time continuing? I didn't believe it. The high tower, rising like a lighthouse in a sea of mist, was inaccessible to reality. Even the birds flung themselves about as though there were no trees, no earth to settle on.

I had been married for twenty-four years, more than half my life. The children who were born during my first wedding night now walked heavily about, frowning, groping in worn handbags for small change; their clothes were beginning to grow old and many of them must have stopped falling in love. I found it hard to understand this, as I found it hard to grasp the idea of distance, or as I always found it hard to believe in the actuality of other people's lives. For further proof, there were my own children, who until recently I had loved and cared for. Some were still growing up. Some merely grew thinner or fatter, but the size of their feet, the length of their arms, the circumference of their wrists and ankles would never change, except from disease. In them, in their memories and dreams, I existed firmly enough, however unrecognizable to myself. I stood over stoves, stirring food in a saucepan; I bent and picked things up from the floor; I stepped from side to side in the ritual of bed-making; I ran to the garden calling 'Rain!' and stretched up for the clothespegs, cramming them into one fist and hurrying in, bedouined with washing. I shook thermometers, spooned out medicine; my face hung pinkly over the bath, suspended in steam, while I scrubbed at the free, tough flesh over a kneecap, removing stains. I glowered, frightening, and then again sagged, sank, collapsed with the unendurable labours of a Monday. All this, and more, I saw myself perform in my children's memories, but although I knew that at one time it was so, I could not recognize myself. My children could remember stories of my own childhood, although they found them boring; but I was severed even from those old, clear images which determine, as I had previously thought, everything. The images of my childhood had disappeared.

But on the hill, in the tower, there were no children to identify me or to regulate the chaos of time. It was very light, the glare of the mist more accurate than sunshine. I had taken the telephone receiver off its rest: it lay like an unformed foetus on the table, its cord twisted in thick knots. No postman, milkman, baker or grocer walked on the gravel. The sound of their footsteps, of their low gears grinding up the track, would in any case have been muffled, and I would not have known they were there until they rang the bell. But I was safe. I had ordered no milk or bread, no cornflakes, flour, butter, cocoa, cat food, assorted jellies, biscuits, bacon, honey, cake, salad cream, sugar, tea, currants, chutney, tomato ketchup, gelatine, cream of tartar, soap, detergents, salt, shoe polish, cheese, sausages, rice, baking powder, margarine, orange squash, black-currant syrup, tins of soup or beans or salmon, disinfectant or instant coffee. The women who came to clean, in their fitted coats and Wellington boots, with wedding rings embedded in fingers glazed and pudgy as crystallized fruit, sat home by their fires and cared for their families. Only the wild cats knew I was there. They lay upstairs, spread out on separate beds, with their stomachs heaving and their feet crossed, sleeping as though they were tired.

From time to time I put another log on the fire. I was very aware of comfort. The heat in the tower made irregular, small noises: a sudden thud through the pipes, a creaking, the slow hiss as a log blistered. I sat down again by the window. A man serving a life sentence will never again have children. Capable, strong, alert to love, he stares from his tower and cannot prevent his body growing older. His body is an uninhabited house and the outside walls are the last to crumble. I was alone with myself, and we watched each other with steady, cold, inward eyes: the past and its consequence, the reality and its insubordinate dream.

. . . I bolted the doors and went up to the highest room in the tower. It is all glass, this room, but it was surrounded by cloud, and I couldn't even see the ground. I opened one of the windows and looked down, but I could only see a bed of mist. To be dead would be a perfect solution for me, I thought. But I couldn't bear the idea of pain, the possibility that I would be a broken mess on the gravel, bleating for help. I used to be physically very brave, but now if I pricked my finger I couldn't look at it. I shut the window and went downstairs again. It began to get dark. I wondered whether Jake would come up the hill in the night, when I couldn't see him, or in the day, when the mist would muffle the sound of his footsteps.

ANALYSIS

The whole of this passage is concentrated towards opening the delicate and complicated world of Mrs. Armitage's private suffering to the reader. Yet every shift in emotional balance, every change in attitude, is corroborated and clarified by the tangible world of objects and landscape. Character and location here are minutely attuned to one another.

The description of the tower in the first paragraph sketches what looks, on first glance, like a landscape without figures. But an attentive reading reveals that every detail of the setting illuminates Mrs. Armitage's state of mind. The sense of height, of being above the world, of enclosure within bricks and glass, of the obscurity enforced by the mist and rain, and the apparent dislocation from the ground of the drifting birds, offer an exact image of human isolation. Mrs. Mortimer begins the episode by placing us very firmly in a physical setting; she is not painting a generalized 'mood picture' so much as giving us a precise rendering of a real place with real details. The crispness of her description of the birds, 'like burnt paper', allows us no doubts as to the actuality of the tower. This is an *appropriate*, not a symbolic or allegorical, landscape—a film-maker's location, in fact.

Once that sense of physical, visual isolation has been established, more abstract implications naturally follow. Mrs. Armitage is severed from the world not only in space but in time as well: she has cut herself off from her past. But the speculative tone of most of the second paragraph stays anchored to the physical presence of the tower. 'The high tower, rising like a lighthouse in a sea of mist, was inaccessible to reality'. In that statement the two strains, of abstract speculation and literal description, subtly fuse.

By the third paragraph, the theme of isolation has been stretched to include human identity as well as space and time. Mrs. Armitage in her tower is cut off, first from a sense of 'the actuality of other people's lives', eventually from any conviction of the reality of her own life. Mrs. Mortimer riffles through her pack of visual images of motherhood, letting their cosy domesticity jar against the overwhelming bleakness of the present visual situation where the tower stands alone in a landscape of sky, mist and birds. And the paradoxes multiply as Mrs. Armitage accelerates into her interior monologue. The telephone off the hook—a symbol of disconnection and isolation—looks like a foetus, a child, a reminder of domestic certainty, of the at-oneness which Mrs. Armitage is seeking. The rhetorical catalogue in the third paragraph of the people and things that will not be coming to the tower, brings us sharply back to the physical and material loneliness of the vigil. Throughout the passage Mrs. Mortimer oscillates between extremes: between past and present, between the visual and the abstract, between the cluttered life of a family and the fearful isolation of a woman left on her own to come to terms with herself.

By the fifth paragraph, the tower, which has hitherto been a location or 'objective correlative' for Mrs. Armitage's plight, becomes a kind of metaphor, standing for the woman herself:

> A man serving a life sentence will never again have children. Capable, strong, alert to love, he stares from his tower and cannot prevent his body growing older. His body is an uninhabited house and the outside walls are the last to crumble. I was alone with myself, and we watched each other . . .

The dominant image there is of a deceptive outer casing: the words 'tower', 'body', 'house', occur in such a way as to be almost interchangeable. They are all shells, containing people within them. The people may crumble, but the house, the tower and the body survive. Mrs. Mortimer leaves her heroine a broken woman, waiting for rescue. The tall, proud tower and the crushed self inside it make a dissonant pair. The tower remains as a sort of monument to everything that Mrs. Armitage hoped to be, an embodiment of isolated independence.

I have in this analysis only sketched the interplay between character and setting. How far does the existence of the tower location provide the novelist with a *moral* framework in which to handle her main character? How successfully does Mrs. Mortimer correlate the visual and metaphysical elements in this scene? How many separate functions are assigned to the tower during the course of the extract? How do you think the scene would adapt itself to cinematic treatment?[1]

[1] *The Pumpkin Eater* has been filmed by Jack Clayton from a screenplay adapted from the book by Harold Pinter.

# 10   Character and Submerged Form

Raymond Williams has remarked that the novel, with its immense variety of types, is more like a whole literature than a mere formal genre. It is characteristic of the novel that it is in a constant process of invention: a particular type of story gains currency, lasts for twenty-five or fifty years, then fades. Over the same period new categories will have come into existence and each will probably have only a limited lifespan. The history of the novel is littered with the husks of such temporary forms. The eighteenth-century picaresque novel, the romance, the Victorian adventure story and improving moral tale—all these were appropriate to the conditions of their own time. Sooner or later they became overworked, and for a time were dropped altogether as useful structures. But writers of every period have returned to these apparently burnt-out types, adopting them for an ironic or satiric purpose.

Think, for instance of the relationship between the eighteenth-century traveller's tale and Swift's *Gulliver's Travels.* Swift borrows his basic narrative pattern from the popular sub-literature of his day. He works within a well-worn formula: a rational English gentleman goes on a distant sea voyage and encounters incredible lands, people and customs. But Swift breaks the pattern. In the final section of his satire he discredits Gulliver and reveals that his rationality has led him into a state of hopeless paradox. The effete traditional form has been vigor-ously turned upside down; it lies submerged beneath Swift's reinterpretation, its values twisted and awry. Swift has made us contrast Gulliver's actual behaviour with the kind of expectations aroused by the formal structure. On our reading of other traveller's tales we should expect Gulliver to return comfortably to England, secure in his knowledge that barbarous foreign parts are infinitely less desirable than civilized London. In fact he does precisely the reverse; he discovers that London disgusts him, and aches to go back to the pristine stables of the Houyhnhnms.

In our own time Saul Bellow has tried a similar technique in *The Adventures of Augie March*, where he submerges the form of the 'picaresque' novel beneath his portrait of the rise and fall of a hero in twentieth-century American society. The picaresque form belongs most typically to the literature of the eighteenth century: a free-wheeling hero has a series of adventures which bring him fame, fortune, love and near-disaster. It was the product of an increasingly middle-class society which was just discovering the social and financial possibilities for an individual equipped only with his talent and his wits. Characters like Moll Flanders and Tom Jones exemplified many of the aspirations of their age. Their freedom, their sense of the possibility of things, their capacity to move up and down the social scale, and their cavalier use of money, mirrored back a flattering likeness to their readers. Such heroes may have been villainous on occasions, but their mobility was a quality to be prized and envied. Saul Bellow's version of the picaresque is rather different. On the surface Augie March seems to possess all the required traits— freedom, ambition, lack of scruples. But instead of letting Augie ride high over society, Bellow allows society to corrupt him. The clever and the rich exploit him; beautiful women use him then jilt him. Augie ends up in poverty, married to a kind, but other- wise unspectacular, prostitute.

Probably the best-known recent use of the technique is in William Golding's *Lord of the Flies*. There the submerged form is that of R. M. Ballantyne's *Coral Island*, published exactly one hundred years before Golding's novel in 1854. Ballantyne set a group of polite English schoolboys on a desert island and then demonstrated how their courage, initiative and intelligence produced a model society—a little England in the middle of the Pacific. His book offers a cartoon version of moral British imperialism; it celebrates an age convinced of its own innate goodness. Golding borrows the same basic characters—all well-brought-up prep-school boys—and puts them on a similar desert island in a nuclear age. Opening *Lord of the Flies*, we are led to expect the familiar story, for Golding has adopted Ballantyne's literary manners as well as his situation. The chapter titles, 'Painted Faces and Long Hair', 'A View to a Death', 'Cry of the Hunters', evoke the tone of the nineteenth-century adventure story with its promise of healthy, out-of-doors suspense. But even in the first chapter something seems to be wrong. Some of the boys have diarrhoea from eating the island fruit—a detail unimaginable in Ballantyne's decorous book. Others viciously bully a fat boy with spectacles and asthma. The idyllic situation rapidly degenerates into brute savagery. The children, far from being enterprising young colonialists, reveal themselves as amoral little animals.

The real strength of Golding's novel lies in the way in which it maintains a delicate balance between the demands of the submerged form and its disappointing version of reality. *Coral Island* is not made to seem entirely ludicrous in its assumptions. Ballantyne expressed a popular and fairly reasonable belief in the inherent virtues of civilized man. Golding treats his views with respect, submits them to scrutiny and experiment, and leads the reader towards a reasoned and painful rejection of the Ballantyne thesis. The trouble with mere ridicule is that it tends to be as thoughtless as the attitudes which it is attacking, and one of the dangers of the technique of submerged form is that it can invite the writer to exercise only his spleen and his sense of the absurd.

By way of contrast we might touch on Nathanael West's *A Cool Million*, a novella which is modelled on the 'improving stories' of Horatio Alger, a nineteenth-century American clergyman. Alger's pulp fiction, with titles like *Ragged Dick* and *Tattered Tom*, advanced a naïve belief in self-help and rags-to-riches romance. His heroes, born in the back streets, rose to fame by virtue of their purity and moral industry. Alger wrote for a credulous public; he reduced the American ethic of success to its crudest terms and laced it with his own peculiar brand of sanctimonious Christianity. Nathanael West translated Alger's success stories into a new setting, exploring the fate of the earnestly moral young man in the United States during the Depression era. West drags his hero down into the back streets through a mire of prostitution, violence, theft and rape, until eventually he becomes the mascot of a fascist movement whose badge is the Davy Crocket hat. The contrast is enforced too easily and West's story degenerates into insubstantial farce. West's failure here is rooted in his choice of an original model. The Alger tales were themselves so facile that they afford no real ground for argument or explanation. Consequently West spends most of his time tilting at windmills, ridiculing a form that is already self-evidently ridiculous. The technique of submerged form demands balance and restraint if it is to work effectively. For the reader must be made aware of the tension between the writer's own values and the values implicit in the borrowed model.


## THE MATCHMAKING
### from 'The Magic Barrel' by Bernard Malamud

*A synopsis of the rest of this short story appears at the end of the extract.*

Not long ago there lived in uptown New York, in a small, almost meagre room, though crowded with books, Leo Finkle, a rabbinical student in the Yeshivah University. Finkle, after six years of study, was to be ordained in June and had been advised by an acquaintance that he might find it easier to win himself a congregation if he were married. Since he had no present prospects of marriage, after two tormented days of turning it over in his mind, he called in Pinye Salzman, a marriage broker whose two-line advertisement he had read in the *Forward*.

The matchmaker appeared one night out of the dark fourth-floor hallway of the greystone rooming house where Finkle lived, grasping a black strapped portfolio that had been worn thin with use. Salzman, who had been long in the business, was of slight but dignified build, wearing an old hat, and an overcoat too short and tight for him. He smelled frankly of fish, which he loved to eat, and although he was missing a few teeth, his presence was not displeasing, because of an amiable manner curiously contrasted with mournful eyes. His voice, his lips, his wisp of beard, his bony fingers were animated, but give him a moment of repose and his mild blue eyes revealed a depth of sadness, a characteristic that put Leo a little at ease although the situation, for him, was inherently tense.

He at once informed Salzman why he had asked him to come, explaining that his home was in Cleveland, and that but for his parents, who had married comparatively late in life, he was alone in the world. He had for six years devoted himself almost entirely to his studies, as a result of which, understandably, he had found himself without time for a social life and the company of young women. Therefore he thought it the better part of trial and error—of embarrassing fumbling—to call in an experienced person to advise him on these matters. He remarked in passing that the function of the marriage broker was ancient and honourable, highly approved in the Jewish community, because it made practical the necessary without hindering joy. Moreover, his own parents had been brought together by a matchmaker. They had made, if not a financially profitable marriage—since neither had possessed any worldly goods to speak of—at least a successful one in the sense of their everlasting devotion to each other. Salzman listened in embarrassed surprise, sensing a sort of apology. Later, however, he experienced a glow of pride in his work, an emotion that had left him years ago, and he heartily approved of Finkle.

The two went to their business. Leo had led Salzman to the only clear place in the room, a table near a window that overlooked the lamp-lit city. He seated himself at the matchmaker's side but facing him, attempting by an act of will to suppress the unpleasant tickle in his throat. Salzman eagerly unstrapped his portfolio and removed a loose rubber band from a thin packet of much-handled cards. As he flipped through them, a gesture and sound that physically hurt Leo, the student pretended not to see and gazed steadfastly out the window. Although it was still February, winter was on its last legs, signs of which he had for the first time in years begun to notice. He now observed the round white moon, moving high in the sky through a cloud menagerie, and watched with half-open mouth as it penetrated a huge hen, and dropped out of her like an egg laying itself. Salzman, though pretending through eyeglasses he had just slipped on, to be engaged in scanning the writing on the cards, stole occasional glances at the young man's distinguished face, noting with pleasure the long, severe scholar's nose, brown eyes heavy with learning, sensitive yet ascetic lips, and a certain, almost hollow quality of the dark cheeks. He gazed around at shelves upon shelves of books and let out a soft, contented sigh.

When Leo's eyes fell upon the cards, he counted six spread out in Salzman's hand.

'So few?' he asked in disappointment.

'You wouldn't believe me how much cards I got in my office,' Salzman replied. 'The drawers are already filled to the top, so I keep them now in a barrel, but is every girl good for a new rabbi?'

Leo blushed at this, regretting all he had revealed of himself in a curriculum vitae he had sent to Salzman. He had thought it best to acquaint him with his strict standards and specifications, but in having done so, felt he had told the marriage broker more than was absolutely necessary.

He hesitantly inquired, 'Do you keep photographs of your clients on file?'

'First comes family, amount of dowry, also what kind promises,' Salzman replied, unbuttoning his tight coat and settling himself in the chair. 'After comes pictures, rabbi.'

'Call me Mr. Finkle. I'm not yet a rabbi.'

Salzman said he would, but instead called him doctor, which he changed to rabbi when Leo was not listening too attentively.

Salzman adjusted his horn-rimmed spectacles, gently cleared his throat and read in an eager voice the contents of the top card:

'Sophie P. Twenty-four years. Widow one year. No children. Educated high school and two years college. Father promises eight thousand dollars. Has wonderful wholesale business. Also real estate. On the mother's side comes teachers, also one actor. Well known on Second Avenue.'

Leo gazed up in surprise. 'Did you say a widow?'

'A widow don't mean spoiled, rabbi. She lived with her husband maybe four months. He was a sick boy she made a mistake to marry him.'

'Marrying a widow has never entered my mind.'

'This is because you have no experience. A widow, especially if she is young and healthy like this girl, is a wonderful person to marry. She will be thankful to you the rest of her life. Believe me, if I was looking now for a bride, I would marry a widow.'

Leo reflected, then shook his head.

Salzman hunched his shoulders in an almost imperceptible gesture of disappointment. He placed the card down on the wooded table and began to read another:

'Lily H. High school teacher. Regular. Not a substitute. Has savings and new Dodge car. Lived in Paris one year. Father is successful dentist thirty-five years. Interested in professional man. Well Americanized family. Wonderful opportunity.'

'I knew her personally,' said Salzman. 'I wish you could see this girl. She is a doll. Also very intelligent. All day you could talk to her about books and theyater and what not. She also knows current events.'

'I don't believe you mentioned her age?'

'Her age?' Salzman said, raising his brows. 'Her age is thirty-two years.'

Leo said after a while, 'I'm afraid that seems a little too old.'

Salzman let out a laugh. 'So how old are you, rabbi?'

'Twenty-seven.'

'So what is the difference, tell me, between twenty-seven and thirty-two? My own wife is seven years older than me. So what did I suffer?—Nothing. If Rothschild's a daughter wants to marry you, would you say on account her age, no?'

'Yes,' Leo said dryly.


*Synopsis:* Salzman arranges a meeting between Leo and Lily H., but she turns out to be nearer forty than thirty, and is infatuated with Salzman's picture of Leo as a 'semi-mystical wonder-rabbi'. Leo gives up in disgust, but months later, discovers a packet of photos left in his apartment by Salzman. He falls in love with a snapshot of a girl, and persuades the unwilling Salzman to let him meet her. She is Salzman's daughter, a prostitute. Leo runs to her, clutching flowers, while, 'around the corner, Salzman, leaning against a wall, chanted prayers for the dead.'


ANALYSIS

The title of this story should be enough to arouse our suspicions: there are few occasions when a contemporary writer can use the word 'magic'. And if the title gives us a hint of what is to come, that premonition is fully justified by the opening sentence. Notice how closely Malamud's 'Not long ago . . .' conforms to the 'Once upon a time . . .' formula of the fairy story. As we are introduced to the situation, the parallel is further enforced. The lonely young man in search of a wife is a familiar figure, as is the wise old fairy godfather in the person of the marriage broker. In fairy story terms, we need only the beautiful princess to complete the picture. How far Leo falls short of that goal can be seen in my synopsis of the rest of the story.

By subtly suggesting the form of the fairy tale, Malamud has erected a moral framework which contrasts disastrously with the actual working out of the story. We might label the two major elements of 'The Magic Barrel' as the 'ideal' and the 'real'. The prince-and-princess theme represents the ideal solution to Leo's problem, while the New York tenement setting, Lily H. and the prostitute present us with the hard facts of reality. Throughout the story Malamud very skilfully manages to keep both sides in play, sustaining a permanent and fruitful tension between them.

Malamud sketches his submerged fairy tale form primarily through his handling of language. Consider how he introduces Pinye Salzman in the second paragraph. 'The matchmaker *appeared* one night . . .' The verb 'appeared' obliquely suggests some kind of supernatural manifestation, although Malamud, here as elsewhere, keeps his effects indirect and subdued. When he goes on to describe the marriage broker, Malamud employs the formal, mannered tone of a storyteller:

> His voice, his lips, his wisp of beard, his bony fingers were animated, but give him a moment of repose and his mild blue eyes revealed a depth of sadness . . .

That address to the reader in the subjunctive ('give him a moment of repose . . .') belongs properly to an oral rather than a written tradition of narrative. And Malamud's selection of detail in the actual description of Salzman adds to the impression of stylization: the matchmaker is presented to us almost as a cartoon figure in hard outline.

Later, when the story seems to have found its level in a realistic vein, Malamud surprises with an image that is violently out of key with the general context:

> Although it was still February, winter was on its last legs, signs of which he had for the first time in years begun to notice. He now observed the round white moon, moving high in the sky through a cloud menagerie, and watched with half-open mouth as it penetrated a huge hen, and dropped out of her like an egg laying itself.

The fanciful surrealism of the menagerie metaphor lifts the narrative straight out of the world of gutter realism, and transforms it once again into the high fantasy of fairy tale. Many of Malamud's most successful effects come from putting the reader on a kind of literary switchback: we are constantly being juggled between two arenas of action, never staying in either of them long enough to fully establish our bearings.

For, while the fairy story creates the submerged form of 'The Magic Barrel', it is overlaid by a texture of acutely observant realism. At the beginning of the story, Leo employs Salzman for a thoroughly mundane reason: 'he might find it easier to win himself a congregation if he were married.' The pragmatism of Leo's motive is entirely at odds with the romantic fantasy of the lonely-prince situation. And the story, on one level, is primarily about a business deal. In the long stretch of dialogue between Salzman and Leo, Malamud unerringly catches the tones of salesman and client. Money and family connections are foremost, and Salzman speaks the language, not of love, but of cash and material opportunity:

> 'Sophie P. Twenty-four years. Widow one year. No children. Educated high school and two years college. Father

promises eight thousand dollars. Has wonderful wholesale business. Also real estate.'

Here Malamud's tough realism achieves point and perspective because it is juxtaposed against the traditional romantic setting.

The two main literary styles of 'The Magic Barrel' correlate with the real subject of the story. Romance on the one hand and expediency on the other indicate twin, contrasted ways of marriage. During the story, Leo moves from a pragmatic acceptance of the idea of the arranged marriage to a point where he falls (disastrously?) in love. And in that movement the submerged form of the fairy story triumphantly reasserts itself. The princess may be tarnished, but, amazingly, Leo really loves her. Malamud has intricately balanced his two forms against one another. In that balance, 'The Magic Barrel' bristles with ambiguities.

# Style and Language

## 11  On Discussing the Language of Fiction

To talk about the language of fiction at all is to become involved in the current heated debate between linguists, aestheticians and critics. Our terms for describing the rhetorical characteristics of prose fiction are for the most part limited and vague. Our criteria for deciding how far a novel or story constitutes a distinct 'rhetorical experience' are at present subjective and partisan. One can at best indicate a handful of tentative distinctions and suggest that the interested reader pursue the problem further by reference to at least David Lodge's *The Language of Fiction*, Roger Fowler's *Essays On Style and Language* and Ian Watt's 'The First Paragraph of *The Ambassadors*: An Explication'.

One might begin by questioning the kind of functionalist fallacy bluntly voiced by Ezra Pound in his *ABC of Reading*, 'One reads prose for the subject matter.' Fiction, so the argument goes, is 'about life' and its language has a purely referential status: we read a novel for its story and its insight into character, not for its unique verbal texture. This attitude entails the unrealistic assumption that one can in some way discriminate between the 'subject matter' of the novel and the language used by the novelist to 'convey' this independent entity. But the reader has no power to separate, say, the personal history of Isabel Archer from James's elaborately structured presentation of it in *The Portrait of a Lady*. All we can know of Isabel consists of what James has invented, and the manner in which he renders her character is part and parcel of her character itself. We might argue that a particular sentence sounded implausible, but we could never state that it was untrue. Fiction, by definition, creates what it describes and does not allow us to compare the original subject matter with the partial version embodied in the prose of the novel.

But once we are agreed that language in fiction cannot be treated on an exclusively functional level ('Does the language of this novel *convey* this experience *efficiently?*'), we shall see that the language of a work of fiction bears a complex relationship both to the internal structure of the particular novel and to a variety of external situations. Imagine a single page from a novel, containing a snatch of dialogue, a paragraph of factual narration and a description of landscape. On this page alone several quite distinct types of language are used. The language of the dialogue perhaps imitates the speech characteristics of the kind of people who are supposed to be speaking—it may for instance be in dialect, or adopt some conventional notation for a character's stammer, or insert nonsense syllables to indicate the redundant noise of a real conversation ('er', 'um', 'ahem'). Clearly this language type must be tested for its veracity in imitating a certain use of language outside the novel. The language of factual narrative is of an entirely different kind. Almost certainly it will resemble language used for a similar purpose elsewhere in the novel; it will very probably resemble the language of narrative used by other novelists of the same period and culture. The language of description may display a far greater freedom and bear the hallmark of a personal, idiosyncratic 'style'. If we are going to talk of 'the language of the novel' we shall recognize that the novel contains several or many language types, each of which must be tested against a different set of criteria, while at the same time they are all related to the unifying structure of the complete novel. If we are to describe the dialogue, for instance, on this hypothetical page, we shall refer on the one hand to its mimetic function as an imitation of extra-literary language and on the other to its place within the internal structure of the work ('Why is this dialogue called for here?; What function does it perform in the narrative?'). One also has to take into account the general literary tradition of the particular novel and its relationship to any genre or school of writing. So in discussing a passage from, say, J. D. Salinger's *The Catcher In The Rye*, one would indicate its dependence on language used by New York schoolboys in 1950, its particular place in the theme and structure of the novel and its debt to Mark Twain and other practitioners of American vernacular narrative.

It is important to realize that 'the language of the novel' is dynamic in structure, geared at every point to the development of the narrative. The multiple language types in a single work are granted homogeneity by their relative functions within the whole context. They are related to one another only by the total structure; removed from that structure they appear completely heterogeneous. When one talks, therefore, of 'the language of the novel' one should bear in mind the fact that the phrase is a useful piece of shorthand indicating the governing context, as well as the various verbal patterns in the fictional work. Henry Roth's novel, *Call It Sleep*, offers a good illustration. The book deals with a young Polish boy's initiation into American life at the beginning of the century. David Schearl grows up in New York and moves gradually from the warmth and security of his home to the violence of the city streets; in the process he is robbed of innocence, trust and hope, changing from a sensitive child into a brutalized American guttersnipe. The language of the novel mirrors the deterioration of its human subject. To begin with the narrative is elegant and fluent, but as David loses his grasp of his mother tongue and joins the gang-life of the side-walks, the language becomes increasingly incoherent. The final chapters of of the novel are composed of disjointed fragments of speech, part poetry, part nonsense. At any one point in *Call It Sleep* the language is explicable only in terms of its relationship to the process of breakdown. Single excerpts might be used to demonstrate key stages in the disintegration of David's consciousness, but no passage could, on its own, stand for the dynamic pattern of the language of the novel. Few novels show the links between structure and language as simply and directly as this; nevertheless, the principle applies to every work of fiction, however oblique the relationship may appear to be.

Certain questions present themselves as immediately relevant to any analysis of language used in fiction. What function does the particular type or section of text perform in the total structure of the novel? Is the language peculiar to the fictional work, or is it a mimetic rendering of some extra-literary language usage? Can one discern a personal mannerism or traditional rhetorical system at work in the text? Is there any tendency for the language (for example, by the use of deviant structures or by frequent repetitions of a particular device) to draw our attention to the text as a linguistic object? English literary criticism has not on the whole displayed much interest in specific questions of this kind. Even those critics who have asserted an interest in the language of fiction have frequently betrayed their lack of technical knowledge and terminology; their analyses are often impressionistic at the very points where they ought to be most exact. This is clearly one area of criticism where the precise terminology of linguistics may be valuably applied to literature. Already, perhaps, the future of the field is shadowed by contemporary French criticism, in which Roland Barthes, Roman Jacobson and Claude Lévi-Strauss have indicated the possibilities of collaboration between linguists and critics.


## THREE FIRST PARAGRAPHS FROM RECENT NOVELS

from *Billy Liar* by Keith Waterhouse

Lying in bed, I abandoned the facts again and was back in Ambrosia. By rights, the march-past started in the Avenue of the

Presidents, but it was an easy thing to shift the whole thing into Town Square. My friends had vantage seats on the town-hall steps where no flag flew more proudly than the tattered blue star of the Ambrosian Federation, the standard we had carried into battle. One by one the regiments marched past, and when they had gone—the Guards, the Parachute Regiment, the King's Own Yorkshire Light Infantry—a hush fell over the crowds and they removed their hats for the proud remnants of the Ambrosian Grand Yeomanry. It was true that we had entered the war late, and some criticized us for that; but out of two thousand who went into battle only seven remained to hear the rebuke. We limped along as we had arrived from the battlefield, the mud still on our shredded uniforms, but with a proud swing to our kilts. The band played 'March of the Movies'. The war memorial was decked with blue poppies, the strange bloom found only in Ambrosia.

From *The Sot-Weed Factor* by John Barth

In the last years of the seventeenth century there was to be found among the fops and fools of the London coffee houses one rangy, gangling flitch called Ebenezer Cooke, more ambitious than talented, and yet more talented than prudent, who, like his friends-in-folly, all of whom were supposed to be educating at Oxford or Cambridge, had found the sound of Mother English more fun to game with than her sense to labour over, and so rather than applying himself to the pains of scholarship, had learned the knack of versifying, and ground out quires of couplets after the fashion of the day, afroth with *Joves* and *Jupiters*, aclang with jarring rhymes, and string-taut with similes stretched to the snapping-point.

From *Hemlock and After* by Angus Wilson

Of all the communications that Bernard Sands received on the day of his triumph the one which gave him the greatest satisfaction was the Treasury's final confirmation of official financial backing. He looked back over his long years of struggle and victory, against authority in all the guises which the literary world could lend it—publishers, editors, critics, cultural committees, the reading public—and noted with a certain surprise that he had almost come to take his ultimate ascendancy for granted. The earliest victories, of course, had cost him the most in self-discipline and in intellectual determination. For a Grand Old Man of Letters it had become fairly plain sailing; even, he reflected with satisfaction, for a Grand Enfant Terrible, though he instantly reminded himself of the histrionic dangers—the knickerbockered, bearded, self-satisfied, quizzing air—of the position he had won in English life. If he had forced from the public and the critics respect and hearing for his eternal questioning of their best-loved 'truths', he must never allow them to feel they were indulging the court jester. They should continue to take from him exactly the pill they did not like, and take it without the sugar of whimsy. Beneath his lined, large-featured face a certain bony determination asserted itself as he thought with satisfaction of his proved strength and independence; the habitual irony of his large dark eyes was replaced by an unusual serenity. If on occasion he mistrusted his own powers, it was not a mistrust that he intended others to share.

### ANALYIS

By juxtaposing several short extracts like this one is in a position to see the baffling variousness of language used in novels. Fiction imposes few linguistic conventions, and it is almost impossible to generalize when particular works vary so widely in conception, tone and structure. The tradition of English fiction has never generated a 'fictional language' comparable to the poetic dictions created by the major movements of English verse. We do not even have the equivalent of the French preterite, an obsolete tense in the spoken language which is used to locate narration firmly in the past. Some writers have hewn out a style which is exclusively personal (the multilingual code of Joyce's *Finnegan's Wake*, for example), but most English novelists have imported their language—from other literary works, from their own social or professional environment, from non-literary documents, from a historical or regional milieu—and redeployed it in their novels. The examples here all demonstrate the second type of rhetorical practice: they imitate or echo a use of language derived from outside the fictional work itself.

The first quotation, from Keith Waterhouse's *Billy Liar*, is built out of a sequence of deliberate clichés. The adolescent boy's day-dream is an unremarkable piece of vulgar escapism: he phrases it in the stale language of cinema newsreels, pulp war stories, and sub-Churchillian oratory. The movement of Waterhouse's prose is shaped by this debased rhetorical system: balanced antitheses, platitudinous metaphors ('a hush fell over the crowds'), formal diction ('decked', 'vantage', 'strange bloom'), and a slow, repetitive rhythm combine together to evoke the familiar moth-eaten style of English ceremonial commentary. The very drabness of the language illuminates the character of the boy himself. Billy Fisher's imagination finds its deepest expression in cliché: hopelessly unoriginal, he is defined by his tawdry provincial surroundings; even his dreams of vicarious power are shabby, pompous and curiously dated. His limited resources of language have contaminated him, and throughout *Billy Liar* we watch him submitting to platitudes which eventually incapacitate him, stripping him of the ability to leave the stifling environment of his home town.

John Barth's elaborate pastiche of eighteenth-century mock-epic prose also borrows a rhetorical system to evoke a period and a milieu. The vocabulary ('fops', 'flitch') and syntactical usages ('afroth', 'aclang', 'educating', 'game with') hark back to the English of 1680–1750. Barth's sentence structure is ornately classical and the movement of the passage hinges on a series of balanced antitheses: 'more ambitious than talented, and yet more talented than prudent . . .', 'more fun to game with than her sense to labour over . . .', 'rather than applying himself . . . had learned the knack . . .' Formal rhetorical figures are used generously. Alliterative phrases recur throughout the paragraph ('fops and fools', 'friends-in-folly', 'quires of couplets', '*Joves* and *Jupiters*', 'string-taut with similes stretched to the snapping-point'). The last of these is an absurdly grandiloquent example of sense echoing structure.

Barth's brilliant linguistic caricature conjures up a world and a form so remote from us that it casts an ironic light on the contemporary issues which lie, thinly disguised, just below the surface of the narrative. He is out to explore the unreality of his mode of writing, making the language of the novel counterpoint its subject matter. Facetious optimism, high farce and the existence of a happy-go-lucky comic hero make a strange match with the narrative development of *The Sot-Weed Factor*, in which no one's identity is certain and every character is sustained in a frenzied dance of gratuitous activity. There can be few sensibilities as remote from one another as the eighteenth-century bourgeois and the twentieth-century existentialist; Barth harnesses these two together in an incendiary contrast between language on the one hand and topic on the other.

The last quotation, from Angus Wilson's *Hemlock and After*, is by far the most complex of the three, although it does share certain characteristics with the extracts from Waterhouse and Barth. Like them, it has traces of imitation and parody, but Wilson handles his effects so lightly that his language is inherently devious; it trembles on the edge of explicitness, suggesting, but not finally confirming, a note of satiric mockery. His style here has the slightly-sententious flavour of a *Times* obituary: the achievements of the public figure are elegantly summarized in a vocabulary that seeks to maintain a distance between commonplace reality and grandiose myth. Bernard Sands receives not letters but 'communications' on 'the day of his triumph'; his career moves to an 'ultimate ascendancy' through a smooth rhetorical prose of antithesis and urbane metaphor. The occasional clichés ('Grand Old Man', 'plain sailing', 'take . . . the pill') are part of the common slang of the ruling class, evoking a world of duty, reverence and gamesmanship. The style, and the sentiments expressed, are faintly dull, of unimpeachable good taste, and absolutely final. With few adjustments for individual peculiarities they could be instantly applied to the death of any elder statesman. But the language is given bite and direction by the narrative structure: since Wilson adopts Bernard Sands's point of view, these are Sands's own comments on himself—he is his own obituarist. This ironic shift forces us into a revaluation of both the language and the character. For Sands, the vocabulary of public acclaim has merged imperceptibly with the vocabulary of self-examination, and the elegiac tone of the narrative betrays his replete and confident arrogance.

These examples all indicate one way of viewing language in fiction. They suggest that the verbal texture of the narrative can convey two separate implications: first, the explicit topic referred to by the words on the page; second, the whole social and cultural context of the particular language type employed by the novelist. One of the characteristics of the novel is that it feeds on the social resonance of language: the author is free to explore any mode of writing or speaking known to him, underlining and exploiting its social overtones. Few novels are not, in some sense, 'about' language; in some the writer consciously manipulates the subliminal associations of his medium, in others he is, like Billy Fisher, imprisoned by the unrecognized conventions of the language he uses. To a degree all language functions like slang or cliché: quite apart from what it actually says, it betrays an attitude of mind, an historical occasion and a social context. Much of the value of a linguistic analysis of fiction lies in relating these inevitable properties of language to the particular inflection they are given by the individual narrative structure.

## 12 Registers in the Language of Fiction

The kind of language we use is determined by the situation in which we are using it. The range of vocabulary and syntax available to us at any given moment depends on four main factors: whom we are talking to, what we are talking about, whether we are speaking or writing, and what medium we are using—whether we are writing a letter, an advertisement or a lecture, and so on. These situational segments of a language are referred to by linguists as 'registers'. Each register is suitable for use on only a limited number of occasions: were I talking now to a seminar group, it might be acceptable to say, 'Look, let's sort out this register business so that we can all go and get some coffee.' Since I am writing a book that is moderately formal in tone, that sentence would clearly be out of place: I would be confusing my registers. We are all familiar with the affected manner of someone who adopts an excessively formal register for a commonplace situation. Dickens's Mr. Micawber, for instance, has this to say when he is shown David Copperfield's new lodgings:

> 'My dear Copperfield, this is luxurious. This is a way of life which reminds me of the period when I was myself in a state of celibacy, and Mrs. Micawber had not yet been solicited to plight her faith at the Hymeneal altar.'

Unlike Mr. Micawber, the novelist has a unique freedom to choose any register he pleases without sounding incongruous. He may borrow the language of any situation, however formal or informal, and use it as a medium for fiction. But a register of language subtly changes its nature when it is transferred into a novel. Its new literary context focuses our attention on to the quality of the language and opens the register to more conscious attention than it would elicit in ordinary use. Much the same thing happens as when an *objet trouvé*—a twisted branch, an old bicycle—is placed in an art gallery; we are invited to view the language or the object with a fresh eye in its unaccustomed setting. There is an episode in John Bowen's *Storyboard* when a meeting takes place between members of an advertising agency planning a campaign for a new product. Bowen introduces the scene:

It was in P.A.'s office. Marketing and Media were not present.

One man is referred to by only his initials, while the other two are known, metonymically, by the business functions they perform within the agency. This kind of linguistic practice is, no doubt, part of the perfectly conventional register of language used in the advertising business. But the reader is entitled to take special notice when he meets these expressions in a fictional narrative. During the novel Bowen explores the way in which the commercial structure of the agency has transformed his characters into performers of predictable and superficial routines. The language register of business comes to stand as a symbol for a more deeply pervasive cheapening of the quality of personal life. Where a phrase like 'Marketing and Media' has a very limited implication in ordinary usage, in literature it is allowed to carry its full range of associations, most of which would usually be taboo. As in this example, a literary context is likely to modify whatever registers of language are employed within it.

Many works of fiction adopt a single register and stick to it. The epistolary novel, so popular in the eighteenth century, is built out of the register of letter writing. Samuel Richardson's *Clarissa*, for instance, borrows the distinctive diction and structure of the long, conversational epistle:

Miss Howe to Miss Clarissa Harlowe

Thursday Night, April 27.

I have yours; just brought me. Mr. Hickman has helped me to a lucky expedient, which, with the assistance of the post, will enable me to correspond with you every day. An honest higgler (Simon Collins his name), by whom I shall send this and the two enclosed (now I have your direction whither), goes to town constantly on Mondays, Wednesdays, and Fridays; and can bring back to me from Mr. Wilson's what you shall have caused to be left for me.

As a prose style, Miss Howe's writing sounds a little awkward, perhaps. But its use of conventional formulae ('I have yours . . . the two enclosed . . .') and its breathless, parenthetic syntax have the ring of authenticity: much of Richardson's art lies in his capacity to imitate the tone and style of his characters, even when they lapse, as here, into confusion or inelegance.

In our own time, James Purdy, an American author, appropriates the register of the pulpit in his short story 'Sermon'. This is a partial parody of the famous sermon, 'Sinners in the hands of an angry God', preached by the eighteenth-century New England divine, Jonathan Edwards. But in Purdy's hands, the words turn out to be spoken by God himself:

I am the only thing there is under the circumstances, but you reject me, and why—well I will tell you why. Because you have nothing better to do or be than the person you are now, occupying the particular chair you now occupy and which you are not improving by occupying. You have improved nothing since you came into this situation. You have tried to improve yourself, of course, or things connected with yourself, but you have only finished in making everything worse, you have only finished in making yourself worse than when you were sent, worse than what you were when you were born, worse even than what you were before you entered this great Amphitheatre.

Just how accurately Purdy catches the general register of the sermon may be gauged by comparing his version with a passage from the original by Jonathan Edwards:

> You hang by a slender thread, with the flames of divine wrath flashing about it, and ready every moment to singe it and burn it asunder; and you have no interest in any Mediator, and nothing to lay hold of to save yourself, nothing to keep off the flames of wrath, nothing of your own, nothing that you have ever done, nothing that you can do, to induce God to spare you one moment.

One could, I think, link the two pieces together so that it would be extremely hard to detect where Purdy left off and Edwards began.

Alternatively the novelist may employ two or more registers, exploiting the dissonance between them for ironic effect. Writers of the eighteenth-century mock-epic form consistently used this technique, shifting from a grandiose heroic style to a colloquial register. Henry Fielding, in *Jonathan Wild*, elevates this stylistic trick into a fundamental principle of structure. He repeatedly supplies us with pairs of words, one heroic and one colloquial, binding the two together with expressions like 'or, as the vulgar call it . . .' and 'in the common phrase . . .' The heroic term is always an evasive euphemism, while the 'vulgar' word reveals the truth. So we are presented with absurdities such as 'As these persons wore different *principles*, i.e. *hats*, frequent dissensions grew among them.' Or, on a rather more subtle level:

> When the boy Hymen had, with his lighted torch, driven the boy Cupid out of doors, that is to say, in common phrase, when the violence of Mr. Wild's passion (or rather appetite) for the chaste Letitia began to abate . . .

Three distinct registers operate here: the ornate classical reference, the politely euphemistic 'passion' (which Fielding ironically calls the 'common phrase') and the unadorned actuality of 'appetite'. Fielding reaches the plain truth by a circuitous route, moving from register to register, each rather less formal and more direct than the last.

One of the natural functions of the novelist is to record the prevailing registers of the language of his own time. Our knowledge of the manners of the past is given substance by the language preserved in the novels of an age. We are, I think, still waiting for a writer who will chart the contemporary registers of, say, advertising and politics, as Colin MacInnes in *City of Spades* gave us an authentic version of the language of the London underworld in the nineteen fifties. The example for this chapter is taken from Vladimir Nabokov's *Pale Fire*, where Nabokov brilliantly explores the manner of scholarly commentary, adapting the register of academic language for the purpose of an epic joke at the expense of, among other things, literary criticism.

## EXTRACTS
### from *Pale Fire* by Vladimir Nabokov

*Pale Fire* consists of an autobiographical poem 'Pale Fire' by an imaginary American poet called John Shade, to which Charles C. Kinbote, a refugee scholar from Eastern Europe has added nearly eighty thousand words of 'commentary'. Kinbote, as we learn from the notes to the poem, is the deposed king of Zembla, whom the communist Nova Zemblyans tried to assassinate by means of their hired gunman, Gradus. Gradus succeeded only in killing Shade, and Kinbote publishes 'Pale Fire' after Shade's death with voluminous notes to 'explicate' the poem.

*Extract from the poem 'Pale Fire':*

    For as we know from dreams it is so hard
590 To speak to our dear dead! They disregard

Our apprehension, queaziness and shame—
The awful sense that they're not quite the same.
And our school chum killed in a distant war
Is not surprised to see us at his door,
And in a blend of jauntiness and gloom
Points at the puddles in his basement room.

But who can teach the thoughts we should roll-call
When morning finds us marching to the wall
Under the stage direction of some goon
600 Political, some uniformed baboon?
We'll think of matters only known to us—
Empires of rhyme, Indies of calculus;
Listen to distant cocks crow, and discern
Upon the rough gray wall a rare wall fern;
And while our royal hands are being tied,
Taunt our inferiors, cheerfully deride
The dedicated imbeciles, and spit
Into their eyes just for the fun of it.

Nor can one help the exile, the old man
610 Dying in a motel, with the loud fan
Revolving in the torrid prairie night
And, from the outside, bits of coloured light
Reaching his bed like dark hands from the past
Offering gems; and death is coming fast.
He suffocates and conjures in two tongues
The nebulae dilating in his lungs.

*Extract from Kinbote's Commentary:*
Line 596: Points at the puddles in his basement room

We all know those dreams in which something Stygian soaks through and Lethe leaks in the dreary terms of defective plumbing.

Following this line, there is a false start preserved in the draft
—and I hope the reader will feel something of the chill that
ran down my long and supple spine when I discovered this
variant:

> Should the dead murderer try to embrace
> His outraged victim whom he now must face?
> Do objects have a soul? Or perish must
> Alike great temples and Tanagra dust?

The last syllable of 'Tanagra' and the first three letters of 'dust'
form the name of the murderer whose *shargar* (puny ghost) the
radiant spirit of our poet was soon to face. 'Simple chance!'
the pedestrian reader may cry. But let him try to see, as I have
tried to see, how many such combinations are possible and
plausible. 'Leningrad used to be Petrograd?' 'A prig rad (obs.
past tense of read) us?'

This variant is so prodigious that only scholarly discipline and
a scrupulous regard for the truth prevented me from inserting
it here, and deleting four lines elsewhere (for example, the weak
lines 627–630) so as to preserve the length of the poem.

Shade composed these lines on Tuesday, July 14th. What was
Gradus doing that day? Nothing. Combinational fate rests on
its laurels. We saw him last on the later afternoon of July 10th
when he returned from Lex to his hotel in Geneva, and there we
left him.

For the next four days Gradus remained fretting in Geneva.
The amusing paradox with these men of action is that they
constantly have to endure long stretches of otiosity that they are
unable to fill with anything, lacking as they do the resources of
an adventurous mind. As many people of little culture, Gradus
was a voracious reader of newspapers, pamphlets, chance leaflets
and the multilingual literature that comes with nose drops and

digestive tablets; but this summed up his concessions to intellectual curiosity, and since his eyesight was not too good, and the consumability of local news not unlimited, he had to rely a great deal on the torpor of sidewalk cafés and on the makeshift of sleep.

How much happier the wide-awake indolents, the monarchs among men, the rich monstrous brains deriving intense enjoyment and rapturous pangs from the balustrade of a terrace at nightfall, from the lights and the lake below, from the distant mountain shapes melting into the dark apricot of the afterglow, from the black conifers outlined against the pale ink of the zenith, and from the garnet and green flounces of the water along the silent, sad, forbidden shoreline. Oh my sweet Boscobel! And the tender and terrible memories, and the shame, and the glory, and the maddening intimations, and the star that no party member can ever reach.

On Wednesday morning, still without news, Gradus telegraphed headquarters saying that he thought it unwise to wait any longer and that he would be staying at Hotel Lazuli, Nice.

Lines 597–608: the thoughts we should roll-call, etc.

This passage should be associated in the reader's mind with the extraordinary variant given in the preceding note, for only a week later Tanagra dust and 'our royal hands' were to come together, in real life, in real death.

Had he not fled, our Charles II might have been executed; this would have certainly happened had he been apprehended between the palace and the Rippleson Caves; but he sensed those thick fingers of fate only seldom during his flight; he sensed them feeling for him (as those of a grim old shepherd checking a daughter's virginity) when he was slipping, that night, on the damp ferny flank of Mt. Mandevil (see note to line 149), and next day, at a more eerie altitude, in the heady blue, where the mountaineer becomes aware of a phantom companion. Many times that night our King cast himself upon the ground with the desperate resolution of resting there till dawn that he might shift with less torment what hazard soever he ran. (I am thinking of yet another Charles, another long dark man above two yards high.) But it was all rather physical, or neurotic, and I know perfectly well that my King, if caught and condemned and led away to be shot, would have behaved as he does in lines 606–608: thus he would look about him with insolent composure, and thus he would

> Taunt our inferiors, cheerfully deride
> The dedicated imbeciles and spit
> Into their eyes just for the fun of it

Let me close this important note with a rather anti-Darwinian aphorism: The one who kills is *always* his victim's inferior.

Line 603: Listen to distant cocks crow

One will recall the admirable image in a recent poem by Edsel Ford:

> And often when the cock crew, shaking fire
> Out of the morning and the misty mow

A mow (in Zemblan *muwan*) is the field next to a barn.

Lines 609–614: Nor can one help, etc.

This passage is different in the draft:

> 609   Nor can one help the exile caught by death
> In a chance inn exposed to the hot breath
> Of this America, this humid night:
> Through slatted blinds the stripes of coloured light
> Grope for his bed—magicians from the past
> With philtered gems—and life is ebbing fast.

This describes rather well the 'chance inn', a log cabin, with a tiled bathroom, where I am trying to co-ordinate these notes. At first I was greatly bothered by the blare of diabolical radio music from what I thought was some kind of amusement park across the road—it turned out to be camping tourists—and I was thinking of moving to another place, when they forestalled me. Now it is quieter, except for an irritating wind rattling through the withered aspens, and Cedarn is again a ghost town, and there are no summer fools or spies to stare at me, and my little blue-jeaned fisherman no longer stands on his stone in the stream, and perhaps it is better so.

Line 615: two tongues

English and Zemblan, English and Russian, English and Lettish, English and Estonian, English and Lithuanian, English and Russian, English and Ukrainian, English and Polish, English and Czech, English and Russian, English and Hungarian, English and Rumanian, English and Albanian, English and Bulgarian, English and Serbo-Croatian, English and Russian, American and European.


**ANALYSIS**

Between 1950 and 1957 (*Pale Fire* was published in 1962) Nabokov was writing a translation with commentary of Pushkin's *Eugene Onegin*. His complete work occupies four volumes, of which only a part of the first is taken up by Pushkin's poem. Clearly Nabokov's role as Pushkin-scholar gave him a model for *Pale Fire*, another edited poem with a voluminous commentary. In his foreword to the commentary on *Eugene Onegin* Nabokov observes that, 'among these comments, the reader will find remarks on various textual, lexical, biographical and local matters'. By the time Nabokov became engaged in the self-parody of *Pale Fire*, the biographical and local matters had taken charge, in the form of a splendid digression of epic dimensions.

The whole novel, as this extract shows, is an extended imitation of scholarly modes of procedure, an elaborate language-game involving multiple registers and an acute ear for the nuances of academic and poetic style. The first register we encounter is that of a particular formalized genre of American poetry. The tone of 'Pale Fire' echoes that of the conversational, semi-philosophical poems of Robert Frost and his imitators. Its language is deliberately flat to the point of banality, catching the inflexions of the speaking voice with a dull and predictable accuracy:

> The awful sense that they're not quite the same.
> And our school chum killed in a distant war
> Is not surprised to see us at his door . . .

John Shade here is a poet of the home-baked school, offering us cracker-barrel wisdom with the arch air of the rural philosopher. At the same time he is a devotee of the technique of 'menace by vagueness' in which violence is hinted at by means of language so unspecific and generalized that it could mean almost anything one cared to impute to it. Connoisseurs of W. H. Auden's less satisfactory effects will immediately recognize the source behind:

> Reaching his bed like dark hands from the past
> Offering gems; and death is coming fast.
> He suffocates and conjures in two tongues
> The nebulae dilating in his lungs.

Just what 'nebulae' is doing in the last line is anybody's guess, but it hits off the exact tone of importunate resonance (and affected, semi-scientific terminology) met in so many poems of the period and convention.

In the commentary to the poem, Charles Kinbote exercises the rights of the scholarly elucidator with wild abandon. Little of the commentary properly pertains to the poem, and Kinbote uses the 'textual note' as an invitation to indulge in autobiography, invoking the entire history and geography of his native country Zembla. The poem is not, of course, about Zembla, but Kinbote considers that it ought to have been. As the notes become increasingly irrelevant to the poem, we are launched into the complex personal story of Kinbote's exile, his relationship with Shade, his attempts to persuade Shade to write a 'Zemblan' poem, and his pursuit by the gunman Gradus.

The notes combine a variety of registers—textual criticism, philosophical observation, detective story—but they remain rooted in the tone of Nabokov's commentary on Pushkin. His 'real' scholarship is surprisingly informal, delving into reminiscence and speculation, and *Pale Fire* follows that pattern. Here for comparison is one of Nabokov's notes to *Eugene Onegin*:

> 13/promenaded/ *gulyal: Gulyat'* has not only the sense of 'to stroll,' 'to saunter,' but also 'to go on a spree.' From June, 1817, when he graduated from the Lyceum, to the beginning of May, 1820, Pushkin led a rake's life in Petersburg (interrupted, in 1817 and 1819, by two summer sojourns at his mother's country estate, Mihaylovskoe, province of Pskov). See n. to One: LV: 12.

Once one has grasped Nabokov's rather esoteric view of what is relevant in a textual commentary, it is easy to see just how true to Nabokov's own scholastic style are the notes to *Pale Fire*. Standard expressions in the academic vocabulary jostle with humorous asides and historical remarks. 'Draft', 'variant', 'our poet', are frequent phrases, and there are learned comments on linquistic features: 'A prig *rad* (obs. past tense of read) us?' and 'A mow (in Zemblan *muwan*) is the field next to a barn.'

Nabokov is able to catch the tone of a language register in a single sentence. The last paragraph of the first note, for instance, picks up the terse phrasing of the thriller with absolute precision. Gradus telegraphing his headquarters is a perfect Mickey Spillane character, observed in a language of tough understatement. Or, rather later, when Kinbote describes his flight from Zembla, the narrative achieves the formal eloquence of epic:

> Many times that night our King cast himself upon the ground with the desperate resolution of resting there till dawn that he might shift with less torment what hazard soever he ran.

Why does Nabokov play these virtuoso games with language? Is *Pale Fire* merely a very skilful joke? The questions are difficult ones (raised in most of the original reviews of the novel), but one can try a tentative answer. During the poem 'Pale Fire' Shade writes: '*Man's life as commentary to abstruse/Unfinished poem*. Note for further use.' The 'life' in that couplet is, of course, Charles Kinbote's. It comes across to us in diverse fragments, and as the registers of language change, so we see Kinbote as scholar, hero, victim of a bizarre plot, armchair philosopher and lonely exile. His 'life' has the disorganized, cumbersome quality of the scholarly notes themselves, and Nabokov's unusual fictional form endows the comically sad figure of Kinbote with touching authenticity.

## 13  The Syntax of Fiction

The syntactical structure of any utterance forms a substantial part of the 'information' conveyed by that utterance. Consider the arrangement of clauses in this simple opening to a story:

> Once upon a time there was a princess. And the princess lived in a castle with her mother and father. Her mother and father were King and Queen of the country. One day the king took the princess away on his horse and they rode over the hills and then they came to a great city. . . .

The syntax is coordinate; each independent clause is linked to the next with an 'and' or a 'then', so that the story is presented like a collection of beads threaded on to a string. There is an obvious tendency for the information to come through to us in a series of indigestible gobbets; this effect is offset to some extent by the way in which phrases are repeated from one clause to the next, supplying a basic rhythm and continuity to the anecdote. But syntax enforces no logical subordination between the ideas conveyed in the language; we are invited to view them as perceptually isolated statements. In this example the reason for the coordinate structure is clear: the story has been written to be spoken aloud and the simplest syntax is necessary if the child-listener is to grasp what is going on. But simple syntax can perform a sophisticated function, as in the verse from *Genesis*:

> And God said, Let there be light: and there was light.

The mystery of the creation is rendered by a coordinate, noncausal syntax. The relationship between God's command and the instant appearance of light is inexplicable: no dependent logic can be assigned to a miracle.

By way of complete contrast let us look at an extract from A. J. Ayer's *The Problem of Knowledge*:

> The mistaken doctrine that knowing is an infallible state of mind may have contributed to the view, which is sometimes held, that the only statements that it is possible to know are those that are themselves in some way infallible. The ground for this opinion is that if one knows something to be true one cannot be mistaken. As we remarked when contrasting knowledge with belief, it is inconsistent to say 'I know but I may be wrong'. But the reason why this is inconsistent is that saying 'I know' offers a gurantee which saying 'I may be wrong' withdraws.

The syntax of Ayer's prose is as closely logical as the argument it conveys. The main clause in each sentence is hedged about with subordinate clauses and phrases. The whole structure of the passage is causative and clauses of consequence beginning with the word 'that' are more frequent than any other type. Unlike the narrator of the fairy story Ayer is not so much interested in telling or describing as in explaining. His syntax expresses the web of rational relationships between a complex group of ideas where the syntax of my first quotation expressed the relationships between a series of events in time.

We might usefully think of a writer's syntax as a system which conveys the dynamics of his perception, indicating how his experience is apprehended as well as what that experience is. Once one has identified the general syntactic design of a piece of prose, noticing the writer's stress on particular grammatical features and his use of any deviant structures, one has come a long way towards describing the inherent relationships between the various constituents of the writer's world. Consider, for example, this passage from Ernest Hemingway's short story 'The Big Two-Hearted River':

> Nick laid the bottle full of jumping grasshoppers against a pine trunk. Rapidly he mixed some buckwheat flour with water and stirred it smooth, one cup of flour, one cup of water. He put a handful of coffee in the pot and dipped a lump of grease out of a can and slid it sputtering across the hot skillet. On the smoking skillet he poured smoothly the buckwheat batter. It spread like lava, the grease spitting sharply. Around the edges the buckwheat cake began to firm, then brown, then crisp.

Here is a catalogue of precisely annotated physical actions held within a coordinate syntactical framework. Each item is isolated and presented as an independent object; we are invited to respond to a series of quite separate sensations. The passage maintains a rhythm by repeating the names of focal objects and modifiers ('buckwheat', 'skillet', 'hot-smoking', 'smooth-smoothly', 'sputtering-spitting'). Notice too how Hemingway places his adverbs: twice he inverts conventional word-order ('rapidly he mixed', 'poured smoothly the buckwheat batter'); once he uses an adverb as an adjective ('slid it sputtering'). These slight syntactical deviations help to underline the importance of the adverbs themselves; they stress the dominant mood of movement and activity. The general bareness of Hemingway's syntax reflects his economical and accurate process of perception, creating a rigorous prose centred on actions and objects. The world which it renders is not ordered or explained, for it consists of random, isolated phenomena, intense in themselves but bearing little causal relationship to one another. Compare Hemingway's simple fragmentary landscape with this passage from Jane Austen's *Emma*, in which Emma tries to come to terms with Mr. Knightley's dislike of Frank Churchill:

To take a dislike to a young man, only because he appeared to be of a different disposition from himself, was unworthy the real liberality of mind which she was always used to acknowledge in him; for with all the high opinion of himself, which she had often laid to his charge, she had never before for a moment supposed it could make him unjust to the merit of another.

Emma herself is disturbed and her syntax mirrors her confusion. She is anxious to retain her respect for Mr. Knightley on the one hand and to reject his judgement of Frank Churchill on the other. Emma's natural response to the situation is to endow it with uncertainties, hastily modifying each judgement as soon as she has made it, and retreating into a hazy indirectness of thought and expression. That single long sentence has two main clauses garnished with no fewer than four subordinate clauses and two subordinate phrases. Structurally the passage bears a superficial resemblance to the earlier quotation from *The Problem of Knowledge*. But whereas Ayer's subordinate syntax was governed by a developing idea of real complexity, Emma's thoughts have only the appearance of logic. They form a smokescreen of delusory rationalization where the process of deduction and qualification becomes more important than the reality of the situation which it purports to explain. Emma leaves almost no linguistic stone unturned in her efforts to create a spurious justification for her ambivalent loyalties. The two main clauses reveal the essential content of her feeling: Mr. Knightley's opinions are unworthy of Emma's image of Mr. Knightley, and Emma is surprised to discover that he has not measured up to her predictions. We might reasonably deduce from this that the passage should be concerned with Emma's flawed estimation of another person's character. But it is not. Instead, Emma tries desperately to substantiate her original valuation by arguing that Mr. Knightley's dislike of Frank Churchill is inconsistent with his 'real' character as imagined by Emma herself. Such are the needs of personal vanity. Emma does her best to objectify her prejudices: the subordinate clauses and phrases have the tone of considered and dispassionate judgements. Emma evades directness by constructing elaborate locutions which veil her true meaning. She shies away from verbs, putting in their place a nominal (noun-based) phrase ('for with all the high opinion of himself' instead of 'although he had a high opinion of himself') or a phrase built on an infinitive ('To take a dislike to a young man' in place of 'he disliked Frank Churchill'). Most of the clauses are pompously indirect, never using one word when two can be found. The machinery of syntactical logic meanwhile grinds away vaguely and reassuringly. Emma finds herself to be and easy object of consolation.

Sometimes a prose style is characterized by the writer's repeated use of a particular syntactic feature. The following quotation, taken from *The Hamlet* by William Faulkner, largely derives its effect from the way in which it slips from participle to participle, sustaining an impression of continuous motion:

> Then the wagons would begin to come into sight, drawn up in line at the roadside, the smaller children squatting in the wagons, the women still sitting in the splint chairs in the wagon beds, holding the infants and nursing them when need arose, the men and larger children standing quietly along the ruined and honeysuckle-choked iron fence, watching Armstid as he spaded the earth steadily down the slope of the old garden.

### THE FLIGHT FROM PARIS
from *Jerusalem The Golden* by Margaret Drabble

*Clara, a provincial girl from Northam, Yorkshire, is a postgraduate student at London University. She became infatuated by the Denhams, a rich, literary,*

*Hampstead family, and fell in love with the unhappily-married Gabriel Denham. After spending the week in Paris with him, she packs her bags in the small hours of the morning and prepares to fly back to England by herself. ('Jerusalem The Golden'—'What social joys are there'—is the milieu inhabited by the Denhams, a world of infinite, and sophisticated, possibility.)*

She walked to the Air Terminal at the Invalides. It did not take her as long as she had thought it would, and she was there well before seven. She was on the point of buying herself a bus ticket to Orly when she thought of looking at her plane ticket, and discovered that for some reason it was booked from Le Bourget, so she bought one for Le Bourget instead. It all seemed very simple. It seemed too simple. She wondered why journeys had always seemed so significant before, so fraught with possible disaster. She felt strangely clear and light: weightless, almost. Acts that would once have driven her into a panic of hesitation seemed to have become transformed into simplicity itself, and whole moral inheritance of doubt had dropped away from her; the thought that she might have gone to Orly by mistake did not stay with her, a nagging reminder of human error, an indictment of human effort, but instead it fell calmly away, and drifted off into unnecessary space. She got onto the bus, and sat there with a kind of placid blankness; the night was over, and nothing seemed to be of much importance, it had all grown out into some clear dawn of acceptability.

As the bus moved off, and drove north through Paris to the dreadful outskirts, she realized that she was going to feel ill, and that the night would be in one sense at least paid for, but as she contemplated her growing nausea she found she did not care about it at all, she did not at all care if she was going to be sick all over the bus. It was all the same to her. She stared out of the window, at dirty streets and shabby houses and cemeteries and reaching, unfinished fly-overs, and she thought that she did not care what greeted her when she returned to England, nor what should happen to her, ever, in the future. And yet such carelessness did not pain her; she felt free, the light weight of her limbs, the clear grey spaces in her head, the ebbing of her need, these were merely symptoms of her freedom, and she was in some open early region where despair and hope seemed, as words, quite interchangeable, where she seemed to sit, quite calmly, beside her own fate.

When the bus arrived at Le Bourget, she got off it and went straight to the nearest Ladies' Room and was sick in the wash bowl. She did not give it so much as a thought. Then she washed her face, and her hands, and the bowl, and looked at herself in the mirror, and thought that she did not look too bad; her shirt, which she had been wearing for twenty-four hours, was looking a little dirty, but not on the other hand particularly dirty, not dirtier than it had looked on various more innocent occasions, not dirty enough for anyone to know. She did not look as though she had been up all night; she looked no worse than anyone else, at that early morning hour. She put some lipstick on, and she thought that her face took on a positively radiant aspect from so small an addition; she looked as well as she ever looked, after no matter how many hours of preparation. The complete equality of all actions assailed her, solaced her; there was really no difference, it was all the same, Orly, Le Bourget, lipstick, no lipstick, sleep, no sleep, none of it seemed to matter. It would not even matter, she thought, if Gabriel should come. She wandered out of the Ladies' Room, and went to the desk to acquire her flight ticket, and there she was told that she had to pay seven francs tax for the use of the airport facilities. She looked in her bag, and found that she had six francs fifty change from her ten franc note; the bus had cost her three francs fifty. So she looked at the girl behind the desk, the girl in uniform, and said that she hadn't any money, that she couldn't pay. And as she said it, she could not tell whether she cared so little because the question was so totally uninteresting to her, or whether it was the most interesting thing that had happened to her in her life. The girl behind the desk said that she had to pay, and Clara said once more that she couldn't, and gave her the six fifty, and then started to look in her coat pocket, and found a ten cent bit, and another one, and then she opened her hand bag and looked in the bottom of her hand bag, and found another five cents. She handed them over, and stared at the girl in uniform, and said, 'If I owe you twenty-five cents, does that mean I can't go on the aeroplane?' And all the time the extraordinary flavour of nonchalance, a taste stranger than the taste of celebration from the day before, filled her mouth. It satisfied her, to find herself reduced to the small change of life, to find years of inherited thrift and anxiety and foresight so squarely confronted, with so little disaster in the air. The girl was just suggesting that Clara should look through her bag once more, when a woman standing at the next desk leaned over and gave Clara twenty-five cents, saying '*Je vous en prie, je vous en prie*', and Clara took them and smiled politely, gracelessly liberated from gratitude, and obtained her boarding ticket, and went and sat down on a plastic covered seat to await, in destitution, the announcement of her flight. And she felt, as she waited, that she had perhaps done to herself what she had been trying for years to do to herself: she had cut herself off forever, and she could drift now, a flower cut off from its root, or a seed perhaps, an airy seed dislodged, she could drift now without fear of settling ever again upon the earth.

She took the flight to London as though she flew to London every day, released from all action by her entire poverty, got off the plane, and collected her luggage, and walked to the bus, as though she had been born to such events. She thought of Gabriel, and she found that her feeling for him seemed to have passed already into the tenuous twilight world of nostalgia; she did not look into the future for his face. She got onto the bus as though in a dream, and took the tube from Gloucester Road to Finsbury Park, and a bus up to the Archway from Finsbury Park and when she got home, she found waiting for her a postcard of the Eiffel Tower from her one-time teacher Miss Haines, a letter from her aunt Doris, and a telegram from Northam saying that she was to go to Northam immediately, for her mother was in hospital there and seriously ill.

## ANALYSIS

*Jerusalem The Golden* often sounds like the kind of domestic anecdote which goes through a catalogue of 'Well she said to him . . . and he said to her . . . and then she . . .' The structure is basically coordinate and most of the action of the story appears in print just as it might have been spoken, with directness and simplicity:

> The girl behind the desk said that she had to pay, and Clara said once more that she couldn't, and gave her the six fifty, and then started to look in her coat pocket, and found a ten cent bit, and another one, and then she opened her hand bag and looked in the bottom of her hand bag, and found another five cents.

The coordinate texture of the narration is accentuated by the way in which Miss Drabble avoids dependent clauses by her repeated use of parenthetic or complementary statements. When she qualifies a main clause (as she does frequently), she simply adds a new phrase to modify what has gone before:

> Her shirt, which she had been wearing for twenty-four hours, was looking a little dirty, but not on the other hand particularly dirty, not dirtier than it had looked on various more innocent occasions, not dirty enough for anyone to know.

Her style has the appearance of casual inconsequence; even an important, and conventionally 'literary' metaphor is adjusted with conversational ease: 'She could drift now, a flower cut off from its root, or a seed perhaps . . .' This technique makes us follow, not just the pattern of ideas conveyed in the narrative but the tone of Miss Drabble's 'voice' as well. Our attention is drawn to the dynamics of the story by this carefully-managed mask of artlessness, so that the breathless, interrupted quality of the spoken anecdote is turned into a conscious literary device.

Characteristically, when the style does become mainly subordinate in structure, as in the second paragraph of the extract, it records Clara's interior speculations, not her external actions. Most of the time Clara is engaged in mechanical activity; when she pauses for thought, the qualifying clauses of more complicated syntax come into play:

> . . . she thought that she did not care what greeted her when she returned to England, nor what should happen to her, ever, in the future . . .

So there are in the extract two distinct syntactical styles: a predominantly coordinate structure which is used to register immediate actions and sensations, and an occasional intrusion of subordinate patterns which reflect the processes of Clara's thought. This is not, I think, either an accidental or an insignificant phenomenon.

One central theme runs through the passage, and it is voiced by Clara in the third paragraph:

> The complete equality of all actions assailed her, solaced her; there was really no difference, it was all the same, Orly, Le Bourget, lipstick, no lipstick, sleep, no sleep, none of it seemed to matter.

All actions are equal, and the connections in the narrative are casual not causal ones. Things just happen in that order; they have no special meaning. 'She wondered why journeys had always seemed so significant before, so fraught with possible disaster.' Clara's world is not bound by logic, or even by organized intention: it is essentially contingent, a region of 'placid blankness' where things follow one another with random unpredictability. Conversely it is a world without surprises, and the affair of the airport tax (an open invitation to a display of emotional frustration) is described with the same neutral factuality that marks the rest of the extract. The only reliable dimension is time; that, at least, goes inexorably on. Meanwhile Clara is free, to drift in a world now shorn of significance, cause and meaning.

Just as Clara is 'free', so the syntax of the novel has a corresponding looseness of structure. The narrative follows the same random patterns as Clara herself, imposing no links of subordination on the fragmentary features of her experience. She lives in an '*and* and *then*' world, not a '*because* and *therefore*' one. Stripped of everything but facts and actions, the simple syntax echoes Clara's liberated consciousness. Nothing has to be interpreted or evaluated; nothing need be qualified. Actions have been literally reduced to a pure grey uniformity. The last sentence of the piece dramatizes Clara's new condition:

> . . . when she got home, she found waiting for her a postcard of the Eiffel Tower from her one-time teacher Miss Haines, a letter from her aunt Doris, and a telegram from Northam saying that she was to go to Northam immediately, for her mother was in hospital there and seriously ill.

In the repetitive phrasing of that catalogue, value has been eliminated. The telegram announcing her mother's cancer is no more or less important than the postcard of the Eiffel Tower.

# 14 Imagery in the Language of Fiction

Imagery in fiction is usually less conspicuous than imagery in verse. A poem works with shorter units of language and nearly always over a briefer period of time than a novel. Where in many poems we are made conscious of the images before anything else, in most prose fiction imagery—when it is present at all—operates as a half-hidden undercurrent, something of which we are only sporadically aware. Our overriding interest in the development of plot and character tends to relegate particular images to positions of minor importance. Generally speaking we pass over them as merely illustrative figures, useful for illuminating an event or a person, but best forgotten almost as soon as read. The novelist frequently uses imagery in a purely casual way, and it is important for the critic to remember this. A single image in a novel—however striking—is often no more than a chance comparison. To make a critical issue of it would be to distort the whole nature of the texture of prose fiction.

But there are exceptions. When the novelist wishes to attract attention to his images, to make us consider them as an integral part of his narrative, he has two main alternatives. Either he can repeat a particular image so often that its frequency constantly reminds us of its presence. Or he can extend it over a long passage, drawing detailed parallels between the object and the thing with which it is compared. In both cases he will be giving his imagery an unusual and exaggerated weight. In this discussion, when I point out the use of images in fiction, I shall be referring to imagery of this kind, where the novelist has obviously gone out of his way to underline the importance of the comparison he is making. It might be a good idea to make this a general rule: too many explorations of imagery in the novel have gone astray by drawing mountainous conclusions from a handful of random similes. If a novelist remarks that one of his characters has a back bent like the bough of an elm, we shouldn't take too much notice. If the illustration lasts over several paragraphs or is made twenty times, we are probably right to investigate.

The most common use of imagery in the novel is made by writers who wish to draw a figurative parallel between the behaviour of their characters and some quality in the external world. Henry James in *Portrait of a Lady* offers a characteristically elaborate example. The novel deals with the education and disillusion of Isabel Archer, a self-assured and independent American girl. Early on in the book James constructs a long-drawn-out image in which he identifies Isabel with the idea of a garden:

> Her nature had for her own imagination a certain garden-like quality, a suggestion of perfume and murmuring boughs, of shady bowers and lengthening vistas, which made her feel that introspection was, after all, an exercise in the open air, and that a visit to the recesses of one's mind was harmless when one returned from it with a lapful of roses. But she was often reminded that there were other gardens in the world than those of her virginal soul, and that there were, moreover, a great many places that were not gardens at all—only dusky, pestiferous tracts, planted thick with ugliness and misery.

James returns again and again to that image. Throughout the novel gardens are important locations and Isabel becomes associated with the best characteristics of a garden—a well-tended, fresh and luxuriant creature. But as she becomes deeply involved with two sophisticated and calculating fortune-hunters, she loses judgement and control. Accordingly, James draws more and more on the converse of the image, on the picture of the 'dusky, pestiferous tract'. Nearly two hundred and fifty pages after the passage I have just quoted, Isabel is on the brink of marriage to a man whom the reader guesses to be a worthless dilettante. James expresses her uncertainty like this:

> The working of this young lady's spirit was strange, and I can only give it to you as I see it, not hoping to make it seem altogether natural. Her imagination stopped, as I say; there was a last vague space it could not cross—a dusky, uncertain tract which looked ambiguous, and even slightly treacherous, like a moorland seen in the winter twilight. But she was to cross it yet.

In an actual reading of the novel the near-repetition of phrase may excite no more than a dim echo in the mind of the reader. But James is making a consistent parallel, illustrating Isabel's state of mind by suggesting a process of natural disintegration: just as a garden left to itself becomes a wilderness, so Isabel is poised on the edge of a moral chaos. James's implications are neither as explicit nor as unsubtle as I have made them seem. In the context of the whole novel the images are sprinkled just heavily enough to allow us to draw our own comparisons. On a first reading we may not notice them at all; subsequently they will delicately intrude, hinting at one of many possible interpretations of Isabel's conduct.

Imagery of this kind which links characters with their natural environment occurs most frequently, as one might expect, in the work of those writers for whom nature represents a meaningful, motive force. For both Thomas Hardy and D. H. Lawrence images of nature are central to the structure of their novels. The reader is repeatedly forced to view their characters as if they were growing things, rooted as much to the earth as to the social world. In Hardy's *The Woodlanders* there is a famous passage where Grace Melbury, who is unhappily married to the worldly Dr. Edred Fitzpiers, returns to Giles Winterborne, a 'woodlander':

He looked and smelt like Autumn's very brother, his face being sunburnt to wheat-colour, his eyes blue as cornflowers, his sleeves and leggings dyed with fruit-stains, his hand clammy with the sweet juice of apples, his hat sprinkled with pips, and everywhere about him that atmosphere of cider which at its first return each season has such an indescribable fascination for those who have been born and bred among the orchards. Her heart rose from its late sadness like a released bough, her senses revelled in the sudden lapse back to Nature unadorned.

Where James drew a fragile and tentative comparison between Isabel and the idea of a garden, Hardy enforces a total identification between Giles and the natural world. In that image Giles *becomes* nature, the human embodiment of the orchards. Hardy's image does not 'illustrate' Giles; it transforms him.

But such imagery, whether 'illustrative' or 'transformational', need not be drawn only from the natural environment. The idea of the subjection of man to the machine has become so common a theme in modern fiction that it has often degenerated into platitude. At its most successful it has usually been treated in a muted fashion; the novelist has created a pattern of imagery which joins his human and mechanical subjects by implication rather than by bald statement. Nathanael West's novel of Hollywood, *The Day of the Locust*, is full of portraits of stereo-typical inhabitants of Los Angeles, people who have fallen for the lure of the movies and in the process have lost all individuality and capacity for genuine feeling. They are observed as creations of a grotesque and artificial world, innocents corrupted into mass-produced monstrosities. Here is West's description of a cowboy from Arizona who plays bit-parts in Westerns:

He had a two-dimensional face that a talented child might have drawn with a ruler and compass. His chin was perfectly round and his eyes, which were wide apart, were also round.

His thin mouth ran at right angles to his straight, perpendicular nose. His reddish tan complexion was the same colour from hairline to throat, as though washed in by an expert, and it completed his resemblance to a mechanical drawing.

It is a damning, or rather a pitiable, picture. But West works obliquely, allowing the image of the mechanical drawing to speak for itself. Like so many other characters in *The Day of the Locust*, Earle Shoop the cowboy is a vivid stereotype, someone who has been reduced to a merely two-dimensional existence.

In cases like those I have quoted, imagery is a vital element in the novelist's technique. It enables him to illustrate or transform his human subject matter, bridging categories, linking people and things, making comparisons that are thematically central to the movement of the novel. But such observations should be made with caution: patterns of imagery are fragile things and the critic must beware of trampling over them or of uprooting them from their context.

## HOWARTH

### from *Flight Into Camden* by David Storey

*The narrator of the novel is Margaret Thorpe, the daughter of a Yorkshire miner. She has left a northern provincial town in order to live in London with Howarth, a married school teacher. Howarth proposes to get a divorce and marry Margaret, but her family are wounded by her behaviour, and she is perpetually uncertain of Howarth's real allegiances. In this extract Margaret and Howarth are together in their furnished flat in Camden.*

I had a habit, when I was lying on the bed and Howarth was across the room, of twisting my head into the sheets so that I could see him upside down. His face then appeared like a piece of apparatus, mechanical and amusingly inhuman. His big toyishness was emphasized by the silent shutting of his eyes and the clamp-like openings of his mouth. It pleased me to be able to turn him at times into a machine, the strange perspective reducing all his humanity to the automatic movements of a puppet or a doll.

Eventually this machine amused me less. For one thing, when he was inverted in this way, and unaware of what I was doing, the real sense of scale would be replaced by an almost infinite one, where his head was nothing less than a mountain, and the great apertures in its side were the features of an indescribable life. They continued to function unknown to him, their mechanism so crude and prodigious that they were unrecognizable: it was an unchallenged, unknown monster in the room with a bloodless, engineering appetite.

I began to be unnerved by this transformation that the mere twisting of a head could produce. Once, when he caught me looking at him in this way, he laughed: the horrible mechanics of it, the great split of his mouth and the huge cogs that were his teeth, the shutter of his eye, convulsed me. The nostrils opened and quivered, the cheeks creased back in thick folds, flushing with the effort of his laughter. The sound itself was transformed into a vibrant mechanical sobbing; the flanges of a great machine rasping together under a heavy load.

I was tormented by my association of Howarth with this infinite mechanism: what was Howarth? When I righted my head and looked at his familiarity, his identity was more elusive than ever. In what way did Howarth occupy this peculiar machine? Where did he end and the impersonal features of his mechanism begin? His physicality depressed me. There was no indication of the margin of his huge male physique, none that I knew I could cross to feel myself in the real Howarth, to be in his individuality, where it lay like a single, hidden egg in the nest of his body. Where was Howarth in all this? And why could he never indicate this division between himself and the mechanism that contained him?

After my father's visit it was as if he took advantage of this obscurity to protect himself. There was a new warmth and intensity between us. Yet there were moments now of deep withdrawal, when I couldn't feel at all that he was with me, as if he wished desperately not to burden me with the thing that he was. My father had exaggerated the wall of confusion and antagonism surrounding Howarth: but at school and now at home he had experienced this open resentment and abuse. One day, when we were out walking in the park, he pointed out a group of children coming towards us, and laughing slightly said they were ones that he taught. They smiled at him as they passed and he called out cheerfully to them. When they were behind us I heard their abuse called after him, full of obscenity and filth, bringing my heart into my mouth. I looked at him. His face had stiffened, and paled. I could have fallen on the ground and wept for him. But he showed no sign except that weariness round his eyes. And we never went in the park again.

Perhaps he wanted to assume all the responsibility for defending me as well as himself. The collapse of the divorce suit, the visit of my father, even Fawcett's coming, had all reduced the sanctuary wall. His need for a vista, for a view in his life, only increased at this sudden widening of his horizon. As I watched his moodiness increase, and that hunted look come into his eyes, I felt that he was concealing himself more and more behind that mechanistic barrier, as if he wished to be absorbed indistinguishably into the vast mechanics of the city around.

When I asked him about this, telling him that I was beginning to feel like some object discarded in his wake, he was immediately warm and disbelieving, coming to hold me tightly, and assuring me physically that there could never be such a thing. 'How could I ever leave you?' he said, laughing at the impossibility.

'Because I was the means of you doing this, of being alone. And now you've achieved it you want to get rid of the means.'

'But that's utter nonsense,' he said with his schoolteacher vehemence. 'Have I ever shown one sign of going back on you? I just couldn't do it. And remember it was you who left me a few days ago. You drove yourself to that.' He was so confident and hurt that I had to be dissuaded from my feelings.

Later I asked him, 'Are you sure she will re-petition . . . can she petition for divorce again?'

But his confidence had already subsided.

'How long will she make you wait?' I insisted.

'I don't know.' He moodily showed he was no longer indifferent to her hold over him.

And within a few days he was saying, 'I never thought I'd be waiting on her beck and call like this . . . I've been thinking— I ought to go and see her and make her realize she must change her mind. I'm certain I could by talking to her. . . .'

'How long would it take? How long would you be away?'

'I might do it in a day, in two days,' he encouraged himself, seeing that I wasn't offended. 'Would you want me to do that? To go and have it out . . . Would you like to come with me?'

'I don't ever want to see her. If you go I'd rather you did it quickly.'

He went the following week-end, as if he'd been waiting a long time for this opportunity. I wasn't sure why he went. There was something more to it than just the need to convince her.

I saw him off at King's Cross still full of the memory of my father's departure: both of us were afraid of the separation, of what there was in it that we couldn't see. For a moment, after the train had gone, disappearing sickeningly into that great tunnel, I thought I'd never see him again. I sobbed wildly as I walked down the platform, with a sudden and brief hysteria: by the time I reached the barrier I was calm. He was making every effort to come back that night, and I knew he meant it. I filled in the day as best I could, walking about town, afraid of waiting alone in that empty flat.

## ANALYSIS

The extract begins with a simple picture, as Margaret watches Howarth from the bed, seeing him upside down. Everything that develops later springs from that initial image. This is typical of Storey's writing: he exhibits a very strong sense of the importance of the visual. It is perhaps worth remembering that he was first trained as a painter, at the Slade School of Fine Art, and he has managed to import into his novels a fine eye for the shape and detail of human behaviour. But he does more than this. He manages his imagery so that it is constantly changing; he elaborates the picture and makes deductions from it, so that gradually a complete small world is built in which Howarth, Margaret and the city are seen to exist in a controlled and meaningful relationship to one another.

Throughout the book Howarth is known only by his surname, a touch of formality that keeps both Margaret and the reader at a wary distance from him. Even in their most intimate moments Margaret is uncertain, and even afraid, of Howarth. When she sees him as 'a piece of apparatus, mechanical and amusingly inhuman', the image is immediately appropriate. To some extent, we have seen Howarth like this all along. But although the analogy begins as a kind of visual joke it rapidly takes charge of Howarth altogether, turning him into an 'unknown monster . . . with a bloodless, engineering appetite'. Storey's mechanical imagery is deliberately generalized; Howarth is seen, not as a particular type of machine, but as a formless embodiment of all machinery. He has the 'shutter' of a camera, cogs, flanges, apertures, and so on. There is little coherence in the picture, for Howarth has to emerge as a machine-monster, something foreign and incomprehensible. Margaret builds up an alarmingly vague portrait, then suddenly ruptures the mechanical description by an entirely new image:

> There was no indication of the margin of his huge male physique, none that I knew I could cross to feel myself in the real Howarth, to be in his individuality, where it lay like a single, hidden egg in the nest of his body.

The intrusion of natural imagery is apt: through the idea of the egg in the nest Storey catches the violent contrast between Howarth's rigid exterior and his delicately protected personal self—the interior which Margaret glimpses but is never able to grasp. In the opposition between the natural and the mechanical, Storey finds a parallel for the distinction between private reality and public front. The first four paragraphs provide us with a key for interpreting Howarth's often baffling behaviour, and in the fifth paragraph Storey creates an encounter which dramatizes the whole issue. When Margaret hears the children calling obscenities after Howarth she 'could have fallen on the ground and wept for him.' But his aloof stiffness prevents her from making any response: he puts up a defensive mechanical shield which forbids even Margaret from trespassing on his private feelings. Howarth's machine-like quality is contagious; it infects Margaret's own capacity to behave humanly or naturally. As she remarks later, 'I was beginning to feel like some object discarded in his wake'. Characteristically Howarth answers her by being 'warm and disbelieving'. He has a talent for self-contradiction, changing without warning from tough mechanicality to spontaneous warmth.

Storey extends the terms of his image at the end of the sixth paragraph. Margaret observes:

> I felt that he was concealing himself more and more behind

that mechanistic barrier, as if he wished it to be absorbed indistinguishably into the vast mechanics of the city around.

That explicit association between Howarth's exterior and the nature of the city is important. It evokes a major theme in the literature of the twentieth century, identifying the city as an agency of dehumanization, of brute mechanism. Is Howarth, with all his wounded defensiveness and sour pride, an inevitable product of urban life? If he wishes to be 'absorbed indistinguishably' into the mechanics of the city, is this not also a desire for self-extinction and the negation of human feeling? These are the kind of questions that underlie the figure of Howarth, and Storey seems to confirm them in the last paragraph of the extract.

The scene at the station is handled with reticence and economy. The simple pain of the separation is treated with the minimum of emotional display. But the occasion is heavily coloured by the imagery which has preceded it, and as Howarth is carried away into the 'great tunnel' one cannot help feeling that he has, at least temporarily, gained the absorption for which he seemed to crave. The impersonality of the railway platform, with its barrier, echoes the detached mechanical front of Howarth himself.

I think it is important to state that the pattern of imagery which I have traced here can be observed repeatedly elsewhere in the novel. The conflict between spontaneous emotional expression and mechanical rigidity is central to *Flight Into Camden* and, incidentally, to the rest of David Storey's work. As on this occasion, Storey frequently creates a body of imagery in order to sketch the outlines of his moral world.

## 15 Irony in the Language of Fiction

H. W. Fowler in his *Dictionary of Modern English Usage* provides a good preliminary definition for a discussion of irony:

> Irony is a form of utterance that postulates a double audience, consisting of one party that hearing shall hear and shall not understand, and another party that, when more is meant than meets the ear, is aware both of that more and of the outsiders' incomprehension.

The real satisfaction of irony lies in that sense of inclusion among the chosen few who hear and are aware. Irony is essentially an exclusive use of language, in which speaker and initiated listener collude in a private communication which debars the uninformed outsider. Yet at the same time the outsider *thinks* he has grasped what is going on, for the ironic statement sounds perfectly plausible in its 'open' form. As A. E. Dyson has observed in *The Crazy Fabric*, 'Satire thrives on moral extremes'. For both the 'open' message and the 'secret antithesis' contained within it must hold good. Simple sarcasm is not irony, since there can be little reasonable doubt about the speaker's intended meaning: When Sergeant Buzfuz, during the trial of Mr. Pickwick, questions Sam Weller about what he saw, Sam replies:

> Yes, I have a pair of eyes . . . and that's just it. If they wos a pair o' patent double million magnifyin' gas microscopes of hextra power, p'raps I might be able to see through a flight o' stairs and a deal door; but bein' only eyes, you see, my wision's limited.

Sam's answer is sarcastic, not ironic. Since not even the Sergeant could possibly think that Sam's eyes constitute a pair of double million magnifying gas microscopes, there is no distinction between an 'open' and a 'closed' meaning. Compare this with a much more ambivalent statement from Thomas Love Peacock's *The Misfortunes of Elphin*:

> As Taliesin grew up, Gwythno instructed him in all the knowledge of the age, which was of course not much, in comparison with ours. The science of political economy was sleeping in the womb of time. The advantage of growing rich by getting into debt and paying interest was altogether unknown; the safe and economical currency, which is produced by a man writing his name on a bit of paper, for which other men give him their property, and which he is always ready to exchange for another bit of paper, of an equally safe and economical manufacture . . . is a stretch of wisdom to which the people of those days had nothing to compare.

The idea of an economy based on a system of credit and paper currency is not self-evidently ludicrous; it is a commonplace reality of some considerable importance. But Peacock makes it sound ludicrous by the ingenuous simplicity with which he describes it, and when he blandly talks of the 'advantage' and 'wisdom' of these procedures, the compliments themselves turn sour. But we shouldn't automatically assume that Peacock wants us to agree with the 'secret antithesis' of his statement—that modern economies are absurd. That would be to concur with a sentiment just as ingenuous as the assumption that such an economy is an unmitigated blessing. Rather, Peacock seems to be exposing the question of the credit economy as a subject of possible controversy instead of as an immutable product of history. Even when we have gauged his irony, the author himself keeps his real opinions hidden. At the very moment when we think we are in private contact with the writer, the irony turns out to have a second barb, on which, if we are not careful, we are firmly hooked.

Peacock's irony lies largely in the peculiar nature of the topic, which he accentuates by his bald description. Sometimes irony is much more a matter of tone and delivery. The characteristic method of Swift, the most accomplished ironist of our literature, is to adopt so sweetly reasonable a manner that we swallow the outrageous statement almost unawares. Here is Swift arguing against the abolition of Christianity:

> First, I am very sensible how much the Gentlemen of Wit and Pleasure are apt to murmur, and be choqued at the sight of so many daggled-tail Parsons, who happen to fall in their Way, and offend their Eyes: But at the same Time these wise Reformers do not consider what an Advantage and Felicity it is, for great Wits to be always provided with Objects of Scorn and Contempt, in order to exercise and improve their Talents, and divert their Spleen from falling on each other, or on themselves; especially when all this may be done without the least imaginable *Danger to their Persons.*

Swift's cause is worthy, and the even balance of his tone is just what we expect of a devout and reasonable man. But his actual reasons are absurd—or are they? The literal content of the paragraph is crudely true: the great wit shows off at his best when he is provided with a stooge on whom he can exercise his malice without fear of reprisal. Nor do the clergy really survive that sneer of 'daggled-tail'; it sounds uncomfortably just. But the full force of Swift's contempt is reserved for the kind of pragmatic reformer who will use any argument or means to achieve an ultimately praiseworthy end: he invites us to ridicule the whole process of his own apparent rhetoric and reasoning. Like Peacock, Swift makes his irony double-edged; he forces the reader to submit to the authority of paradox.

There is a further ironic technique which looks at first sight ·

like simple exaggeration. Evelyn Waugh begins his futuristic political satire, *Love Among the Ruins*, with the sentence, 'Despite their promises at the last Election, the politicians had not yet changed the climate.' The novel continues in the same vein of elegant humour, mocking the Welfare State where society is run on rationally humane principles:

> Euthanasia had not been part of the original 1945 Health Service; it was a Tory measure designed to attract votes from the aged and mortally sick. Under the Bevan-Eden Coalition the Service came into general use and won instant popularity. The Union of Teachers was pressing for its application to difficult children. Foreigners came in such numbers to take advantage of the service that immigration authorities now turned back the bearers of single tickets.

Like George Orwell's *Nineteen Eighty-Four* and Aldous Huxley's *Brave New World*, *Love Among The Ruins* looks like a fantasy. But at some point the reader is likely to become suspicious that things may not be quite as fantastic as they at first appear. For this beneficent state where mercy-killing, free love and unlimited leisure are among the rights of every citizen holds an unflattering mirror up to the ideals of modern humanism. Although the novel is set in the future, it indicts the present. The irony of Huxley, Orwell and Waugh treats fantasy as a means of access to reality: these writers create nightmares which amazingly prove to be the very worlds we are living in.

The ironist is naturally devious; his style, however bland or persuasive, is to be distrusted and we agree with him at our peril. The greatest ironists, like Swift or Jane Austen, still retain their power to resist any kind of assured interpretation. Their tone is so consistently ambiguous that we are forced far beyond the simple recognition of a 'double meaning' into realizing the truth of conflicting values. The surest test of a fine ironist is to ask whether he unnerves and disconcerts his readers.

## THE PROLE QUARTER
### from George Orwell's *Nineteen Eighty-Four*

*In this sequence Winston Smith wanders into the part of London now occupied by the proles, the subject class of the hierarchical society headed by Big Brother and the Inner Party.*

'If there is hope,' he had written in the diary, 'it lies in the proles.' The words kept coming back to him, statement of a mystical truth and a palpable absurdity. He was somewhere in the vague, brown-coloured slums to the north and east of what had once been Saint Pancras Station. He was walking up a cobbled street of little two-storey houses with battered doorways which gave straight on the pavement and which were somehow curiously suggestive of ratholes. There were puddles of filthy water here and there among the cobbles. In and out of the dark doorways, and down narrow alley-ways that branched off on either side, people swarmed in astonishing numbers—girls in full bloom, with crudely lipsticked mouths, and youths who chased the girls, and swollen waddling women who showed you what the girls would be like in ten years time, and old bent creatures shuffling along on splayed feet, and ragged barefooted children who played in the puddles and then scattered at angry yells from their mothers. Perhaps a quarter of the windows in the street were broken and boarded up. Most of the people paid no attention to Winston; a few eyed him with a sort of guarded curiosity. Two monstrous women with brick-red forearms folded across their aprons were talking outside a doorway. Winston caught scraps of conversation as he approached.

' "Yes," I says to 'er, "that's all very well," I says. "But if you'd of been in my place you'd of done the same as what I done. It's easy to criticize," I says, "but you ain't got the same problems as what I got." '

'Ah,' said the other, 'that's jest it. That's jest where it is.'

The strident voices stopped abruptly. The women studied him in hostile silence as he went past. But it was not hostility, exactly; merely a kind of wariness, a momentary stiffening, as at the passing of some unfamiliar animal. The blue overalls of the Party could not be a common sight in a street like this. Indeed, it was unwise to be seen in such places, unless you had definite business there. The patrols might stop you if you happened to run into them. 'May I see your papers, comrade? What are you doing here? What time did you leave work? Is this your usual way home?'—and so on and so forth. Not that there was any rule against walking home by an unusual route: but it was enough to draw attention to you if the Thought Police heard about it.

Suddenly the whole street was in commotion. There were yells of warning from all sides. People were shooting into the door-ways like rabbits. A young woman leapt out of a doorway a little ahead of Winston, grabbed up a tiny child playing in a puddle, whipped her apron round it and leapt back again, all in one movement. At the same instant a man in a concertina-like black suit, who had emerged from a side alley, ran towards Winston, pointing excitedly to the sky.

'Steamer!' he yelled. 'Look out, guv'nor! Bang over'ead! Lay down quick!'

'Steamer' was a nickname which, for some reason, the proles applied to rocket bombs. Winston promptly flung himself on his face. The proles were nearly always right when they gave you a warning of this kind. They seemed to possess some kind of instinct which told them several seconds in advance when a rocket was coming, although the rockets supposedly travelled faster than sound. Winston clasped his forearms above his head. There was a roar that seemed to make the pavement heave; a shower of light objects pattered on to his back. When he stood up he found that he was covered with fragments of glass from the nearest window.

He walked on. The bomb had demolished a group of houses two hundred metres up the street. A black plume of smoke hung in the sky, and below it a cloud of plaster dust in which a crowd was already forming round the ruins. There was a little pile of plaster lying on the pavement ahead of him, and in the middle of it he could see a bright red streak. When he got up to it he saw that it was a human hand severed at the wrist. Apart from the bloody stump, the hand was so completely whitened as to resemble a plaster cast.

He kicked the thing into the gutter, and then, to avoid the crowd, turned down a side street to the right. Within three or four minutes he was out of the area which the bomb had affected, and the sordid swarming life of the streets was going on as though nothing had happened. It was nearly twenty hours, and the drinking-shops which the proles frequented ('pubs', they called them) were choked with customers. From their grimy swing doors, endlessly opening and shutting there came forth a smell of urine, sawdust and sour beer. In an angle formed by a projecting housefront three men were standing very close together, the middle one of them holding a folded-up newspaper which the other two were studying over his shoulder. Even before he was near enough to make out the expression of their faces, Winston could see absorption in every line of their bodies. It was obviously some serious piece of news that they were reading. He was a few paces away from them when suddenly the group broke up and two of the men were in violent altercation. For a moment they seemed almost on the point of blows.

'Can't you bleeding well listen to what I say? I tell you no number ending in seven ain't won for over fourteen months?'

'Yes it 'as, then!'

'No, it 'as not! Back 'ome I got the 'ole lot of 'em for over two years wrote down on a piece of paper. I takes 'em down reg'lar as the clock. An' I tell you, no number ending in seven—'

'Yes, a seven 'as won! I could pretty near tell you the bleeding

number. Four oh seven, it ended in. It were in February—second
week in February.'

'February your grandmother! I got it all down in black and
white. An' I tell you, no number—'

'Oh, pack it in!' said the third man.

They were talking about the Lottery. Winston looked back
when he had gone thirty metres. They were still arguing, with
vivid, passionate faces. The Lottery, with its weekly pay-out
of enormous prizes, was the one public event to which the proles
paid serious attention. It was probable that there were some
millions of proles for whom the Lottery was the principal if not
the only reason for remaining alive. It was their delight, their
folly, their anodyne, their intellectual stimulant. Where the
Lottery was concerned, even people who could barely read and
write seemed capable of intricate calculations and staggering
feats of memory. There was a whole tribe of men who made a
living simply by selling systems, forecasts and lucky amulets.
Winston had nothing to do with the running of the Lottery,
which was managed by the Ministry of Plenty, but he was aware
(indeed everyone in the Party was aware) that the prizes were
largely imaginary. Only small sums were actually paid out, the
winners of the big prizes being non-existent persons. In the
absence of any real inter-communication between one part of
Oceania and another, this was not difficult to arrange.

But if there was hope, it lay in the proles. You had to cling
on to that. When you put it in words it sounded reasonable: it
was when you looked at the human beings passing you on the
pavement that it became an act of faith.

ANALYSIS

Orwell's irony hinges around the title of *Nineteen Eighty-Four*.
Published in 1949, it was composed between 1946 and 1948.

It holds a distorting mirror, not to some distant and theoretical future, but to the politics and social life of the immediately postwar period. The stringencies of war, the austere programmes of the Attlee government, the patriotic chauvinism stirred up by war-time propaganda, these are the essential subjects of this only-seemingly futuristic satire. Orwell was bitterly disenchanted with what he identified as the stale bureaucucracy of British Labour Party policy. He distrusted utopian schemes and preached instead a kind of pragmatic anarchism founded on a conception of personal dignity and liberty. *Nineteen Eighty-Four* is an anguished account of the state of England in nineteen forty-eight.

The novel adopts the point of view of Winston Smith, an average representative of decent liberal attitudes who is terrified and outraged by the cynical politics of The Party. The reader of *Nineteen Eighty-Four* is likely both to accept Winston's responses to the situation and at the same time to find the situation itself incredible. By making us identify with Winston and by convincing us that the novel deals with a nightmare, Orwell baits the trap which he is later to snap shut. The extract offers a particularly fine example of Orwell's ironic method; he initially elicits our sympathy, then reveals how our feelings have been superficially misplaced.

The structure of the episode is simple to the point of being diagrammatic. Conventional socialist dogma, with its insistence on the power and future of the masses, is voiced, tested against an apparent reality, and relegated at the end as a pious but unworkable myth. The final paragraph of the extract supplies a paraphrase of the whole sequence:

> But if there was hope, it lay in the proles. You had to cling on to that. When you put it into words it sounded reasonable: it was when you looked at the human beings passing you on the pavement that it became an act of faith.

The sentiment reached by Winston after his brief and fragmentary contact with the proles is a familiar radical platitude, a favourite parlour dismissal of Marxist theory. But Orwell invites us to consider the process by which Winston arrives at this predictably glib conclusion. Winston's language betrays him, and Orwell develops an ironic counter-statement which undercuts the reasonable surface of Winston's argument.

Consider how the proles are described. Throughout the passage there is a predominance of animal imagery: people are transposed into a primitive gregarious species. They 'swarm'; their houses are like 'ratholes'; they run like 'rabbits'. Winston's attitude towards them is that of a zoologist observing the habits of vermin, emotionally detached and physically repelled. When he tries to define his own relationship to the proles he phrases it in terms, not of class, but of biology: 'a momentary stiffening, as at the passing of some unfamiliar animal'. The language and habits of the proles are so alien that they constitute an independent, sub-human pattern of behaviour, and Winston constantly underlines his ignorance of their ways. They name rocket bombs 'steamers' 'for some reason', and their reflexes are inexplicable to the outside observer:

> They seemed to possess some kind of instinct which told them several seconds in advance when a rocket was coming, although the rockets supposedly travelled faster than sound.

When Winston hears them talking he picks up only meaningless fragments of conversation, gibberish without context or continuation. The first half of the passage is brought to a brilliantly bizarre climax as Winston kicks the hand into the gutter—a terse statement of the total depersonalization of the proles. Up to this point the reader may well have passed over the ironic undertones of the sequence: Winston's reactions have been both credible and not entirely unsympathetic. The incident of the severed hand shocks, not because it happens, but because Winston pays so little attention to it. Paragraphs have been expended in describing Winston's over-sensitized responses to the social habits of the proles, but the meaningless war casualty and its grisly token merit only a casual mention. From this point onwards Orwell's irony becomes open and direct; we are jarred into a circumspect mistrust of Winston's point of view. For as he discusses the drinking shops and the Lottery we are presented with familiar features—pubs and football pools—of our own contemporary landscape, described with the assumed innocence of the classical *eiron*. The technique of this section bears close comparison with the earlier quotation from Thomas Love Peacock's *The Misfortunes of Elphin*. Orwell's writing here has twin functions: we discover that this outrageous dreamlike terrain is, after all, our own world, and we revalue Winston's attitude in the light of this new knowledge. As soon as the passage shifts into broad satire, Winston is revealed as a dupe. His detachment from the proles is clearly only the result of the purposeful class-mystification of the Party state.

Winston turns out to be an unreliable guide to the prole quarter because he acts as a mouthpiece for all the conditioned prejudices encouraged by the very party against which he is trying to rebel. His rejection of the proles is founded on ignorance and he is incapable of penetrating behind the rigid caste categories of the party line. His training and environment have taught him to see the proles as obnoxious animals. He has no capacity to change his own instincts, and is the prisoner of a warped propaganda machine.

The ironic structure of the passage confronts us with a blunt paradox. The proles appear to Winston as alien creatures whose habits arouse a deep-rooted physical revulsion. Yet at the same time this sense of estrangement is inherently absurd, for it is a symptom of the dehumanization of life which Winston and his kind are committed to attack. The barrier of incomprehension is a product of class and culture, even though it manifests itself in biological terms.

Orwell faced but never reconciled this paradox in his own life. In *The Road to Wigan Pier* and *Down And Out In Paris and London* he recorded his attempts to immerse himself in working-class life. His socialism was essentially practical, concerned with specific situations and people. Yet he never managed to shake off his aloofness; even when he was wretchedly poor the vestiges of the Old Etonian still clung to him. Perhaps as a direct result of this recurrent personal predicament, he treats the dilemma of the severance between classes in English social life with bitter sympathy in *Nineteen Eighty-Four*.

The strength of Orwell's irony lies in its fundamental ambiguousness. The narration of this passage is sufficiently persuasive to lead us to accept Winston as an honest interpreter, yet the facts of the sequence reveal a poisoned bias in Winston's attitude. The double view of Orwell's ironic method forces us to accommodate a savage and unbending contradiction.

# Bibliography

*1. Direct Criticism and Commentary:*

ALDRIDGE, John W., *Time to Murder and Create: The Contemporary Novel in Crisis*, New York 1966. An argumentative collection of essays built around the thesis that the contemporary novel is ingrown and emasculated.

ALLOTT, Miriam, *Novelists on the Novel*, London 1959. An important sourcebook in which novelists of all periods write about the problems of their art.

BOOTH, Wayne C., *The Rhetoric of Fiction*, Chicago 1961. A seminal study of narrative technique.

FORSTER, E. M., *Aspects of the Novel*, London 1927. Forster's classic description of the technique of the novelist.

GINDIN, James, *Postwar British Fiction: New Accents and Attitudes*, Cambridge 1962. Gindin discusses many of the authors mentioned here.

HASSAN, Ihab, *Radical Innocence: The Contemporary American Novel*, Princeton, N.J. 1961. A vividly written study of recent American writing.

LODGE, David, *Language of Fiction: Essays in Criticism and Verbal Analysis of The English Novel*, London 1966. A far-ranging and detailed study of fictional style.

LUBBOCK, Percy, *The Craft of Fiction*, London 1921. A landmark in the history of criticism of the novel. Lubbock is a disciple of Henry James and centres his criticism around the idea of narrative point of view.

WATT, Ian, 'The First Paragraph of *The Ambassadors*: An Explication', *Essays in Criticism*, Vol. X, No. 3, July 1960, pp. 250-74. A model exercise in close-reading, Watt's article deserves examination by anyone interested in the nuances of verbal style.

*2. Accessory Reading:*

BARTHES, Roland, *Writing Degree Zero*, London 1967. A 'structuralist' account of the relationship between the language of literature and its social and political context. Particularly relevant to Chapters 11 and 12 of this book.

FOWLER, Roger (ed.), *Essays On Style And Language*, London 1966. Articles by various authors dealing with the application of linguistics to literary analysis, important background material to Chapters 11, 12 and 13 of this book.

LEWIS, Oscar, *The Children of Sánchez*, London 1962. Edited tape recordings of a family in Mexico City telling their own stories. A fascinating blend of literary art and social anthropology.

WILLIAMS, Raymond, *Culture and Society 1780–1950*, London 1958; *The Long Revolution*, London 1961. Williams's two books present a detailed background of social, intellectual and political history. Both are invaluable aids to a study of modern literature in its cultural context.

## 3. Recent English and American Novelists and their Work:

This list makes no claims for comprehensiveness. I have tried to include those writers who seem to me to be contributing most to the contemporary novel. Inevitably there are some invidious distinctions and some quirks of personal taste. I have, for instance, excluded Graham Greene on the grounds that he established his characteristic style well before 1945. Christopher Isherwood, another older writer, is however included: his style has changed so much since the 1930s that his most recent novels strike me as 'contemporary' in a way that Greene's do not. Some writers who are mentioned in passing in the text of the book are not included in the bibliography, while others who are not mentioned at all elsewhere have been given a place. I have tried to use this section as a kind of safety net to catch works and authors whom I have not so far been able to include, but who merit an entry in any description of the contemporary novel. Basic biographical information is given wherever possible.

AMIS, Kingsley, Born 1922, educated City of London School and St. John's College Oxford. Lecturer in English, University College of Wales, Swansea, 1949–1961. Fellow of Peterhouse College, Cambridge, 1961–1963. He is now a freelance writer and lives in London.

Published Fiction: *Lucky Jim*, 1954; *That Uncertain Feeling*, 1955; *I Like It Here*, 1958; *Take A Girl Like You*, 1960; *My Enemy's Enemy* (short stories), 1962; *One Fat Englishman*, 1963; *The Anti-Death League*, 1966; *A Look Around The Estate*, 1967; *I Want It Now*, 1968; *The Green Man*, 1969; *Girl 20*, 1971.

BALDWIN, James, Born 1924, Harlem, New York. Educated De Witt Clinton High School, N.Y. Resident in Europe 1948–1956. Active in the Civil Rights Movement in the U.S.A.

Published Fiction: *Go Tell It On The Mountain*, 1953; *Giovanni's Room*, 1956; *Another Country*, 1962; *Going To Meet The Man*, 1965; *Tell Me How Long the Train's Been Gone*, 1968; *The Amen Corner*, 1969.

BARTH, John, Born 1930, Cambridge, Massachusetts. Educated at Maryland public schools, the Juillard School of Music, New York, and at Johns Hopkins University. Barth has taught English at Pennsylvania State University and at the State University of Buffalo, New York.

Published Fiction: *The Floating Opera*, 1956; *The End of the Road*, 1958; *The Sot-Weed Factor*, 1960; *Giles Goat-Boy*, 1966; *Lost in the Fun House*, 1969.

BELLOW, Saul, Born 1915, Lachine, Quebec, Canada. Educated University of Chicago and Northwestern University. Bellow has taught at a number of American universities, including those of Minnesota, Princeton, New York and Chicago.

Published Fiction: *Dangling Man*, 1944; *The Victim*, 1947; *The Adventures of Augie March*, 1953; *Seize The Day*, 1956; *Henderson The Rain King*, 1959; *Herzog*, 1964; *Mosby's Memoirs And Other Stories*, 1969.

BRADBURY, Malcolm, Born 1932, Sheffield. Educated West Bridgford Grammar School and at the universities of Leicester, London, Indiana and Manchester. Bradbury has taught at the universities of Hull and Birmingham and now lectures in American Literature at the University of East Anglia.

Published Fiction: *Eating People Is Wrong*, 1959; *Stepping Westward*, 1965.

BURROUGHS, William, Born 1914, St. Louis. Has spent much of his life in Europe. Much of Burroughs's writing is concerned with his experiences as a drug addict.

Published Fiction: *Junkie*, 1953; *The Naked Lunch*, 1959; *The Exterminator*, 1960; *The Soft Machine*, 1961; *The Ticket That Exploded*, 1962; *Nova Express*, 1964; *Dead Fingers Talk*, 1966.

CAPOTE, Truman, Born 1924, New Orleans. Educated St. John's Academy and Greenwich High School, New York. Has worked as a reader of scripts for a film company. Won the O. Henry Memorial Award for Short Stories, 1946; elected to the National Institute of Arts and Letters, 1959.

Published Fiction: *Other Voices, Other Rooms*, 1948; *Tree of Night* (short stories), 1949; *The Grass Harp*, 1951; *Breakfast at Tiffany's* (short stories), 1958; *In Cold Blood*, 1966; *The Thanksgiving Visitor*, 1969.

DONLEAVY, J. P., Born 1926. Educated at schools in the United States and at Trinity College, Dublin.

Published Fiction: *The Ginger Man*, 1955; *A Singular Man*, 1963; *Meet My Maker The Mad Molecule* (short stories), 1964; *The Saddest Summer of Samuel S.* (short stories), 1966; *The Beastly Beatitudes of Balthazar, B.* 1969.

DRABBLE, Margaret, Born 1939, Sheffield. Educated at the Mount School, York, and at Newnham College, Cambridge, where she read English. She married the actor Clive Swift in 1960, and has three children. She writes a newspaper column and occasional criticism.

Published Fiction: *A Summer Birdcage*, 1963; *The Garrick Year*, 1964; *The Millstone*, 1965; *Jerusalem the Golden*, 1967; *The Waterfall*, 1969.

DURRELL, Lawrence, F.R.S.L., Born 1912. Educated in India and at St. Edmund's School, Canterbury. Has worked for the Foreign Service and the British Council in many parts of the world. Is well known as a poet and humorist, as well as for his novels.

Published Fiction: *Panic Spring*, 1937; *The Black Book*, 1938; *Justice*, 1957; *Balthazar*, 1958; *Mountolive*, 1958; *Clea*, 1960; *Tunc*, 1967; *Nunquam*, 1970.

ELLISON, Ralph, Born 1914, Oklahoma. Together with James Baldwin, Ellison is probably the best known American negro novelist, although his impressive reputation has been established on the strength of a single work.

Published Fiction: *Invisible Man*, 1952.

GOLDING, William, F.R.S.L., Born 1911. Educated at Marlborough

Grammar School and at Brasenose College, Oxford. Golding served in the Navy during the war, and later taught classics at Bishop Wordsworth's School, Salisbury.

Published Fiction: *Lord Of The Flies*, 1954; *The Inheritors*, 1955; *Pincher Martin*, 1956; *Free Fall*, 1959; *The Spire*, 1964; *The Pyramid*, 1967; *The Scorpion God*, 1971.

ISHERWOOD, Christopher, Born 1904, High Lane, Cheshire. Educated at Repton School and at Corpus Christi, Cambridge. Taught English in Berlin, 1933–1935. In 1946 Isherwood became a United States citizen. Worked as a scriptwriter for Gaumont-British and Metro-Goldwyn-Mayer. Professor of English at University of California.

Published Fiction: *All The Conspirators*, 1928; *The Memorial*, 1932; *Mr. Norris Changes Trains*, 1935; *Goodbye to Berlin*, 1939; *Prater Violet*, 1945; *The World In The Evening*, 1954; *Down There on a Visit*, 1962; *A Single Man*, 1964; *A Meeting By The River*, 1967.

MAILER, Norman, Born 1923, Long Branch, New Jersey. Educated at schools in Brooklyn, New York, and at Harvard. Mailer won *Story* magazine's college contest in 1941 with his short story 'The Greatest Thing In The World'. He served in the United States Army 1944–1946.

Published Fiction: *The Naked and The Dead*, 1948; *Barbary Shore*, 1951; *The Deer Park*, 1955; *An American Dream*, 1964; *Cannibals and Christians*, 1967; *The Armies of the Night*, 1968.

MALAMUD, Bernard, Born 1914, Brooklyn, New York. Educated at Erasmus Hall High School, City College of New York and Columbia University. Malamud is the son of immigrant Russian parents. He has taught literature at various universities in the United States, and has been the recipient of a number of awards, grants and fellowships for fiction-writing, winning the National Book Award in 1959 for *The Magic Barrel*.

Published Fiction: *The Natural*, 1952; *The Assistant*, 1957; *The Magic Barrel* (short stories), 1958; *A New Life*, 1961; *Idiots First* (short stories), 1963; *The Fixer*, 1966.

MOORE, Brian, Born 1921, Belfast. Went to North Africa in 1943, working with the Ministry of War Transport Division as a civilian. After the war, Moore joined U.N.R.R.A. and assisted refugees in Poland, Sweden, Finland and Norway. He entered Canada as an immigrant in 1948, where he worked as a journalist. He now lives in New York.

Published Fiction: *Judith Hearne*, 1955; *The Feast of Lupercal*, 1956; *The Luck of Ginger Coffey*, 1960; *An Answer From Limbo*, 1962; *The Emperor of Ice Cream*, 1965; *I Am Mary Dunne*, 1968; *A Moment of Love*, 1969.

MORTIMER, Penelope, Born Rhyl, North Wales. Educated London University. Has worked as a journalist and written scripts for documentary films.

Published Fiction: *A Villa In Summer*, 1947; *The Bright Prison; With Love and Lizards; Daddy's Gone A-Hunting; The Pumpkin Eater*, 1962; *My Friend Says It's Bullet Proof*, 1967; *Home*, 1971.

MURDOCH, Iris, Born 1919, Dublin. Educated Badminton School, Bristol and Somerville College, Oxford. Was an Assistant Principal at the Treasury, 1942–1944, then worked with U.N.R.R.A. in London, Belgium and Austria. Held a studentship in Philosophy, Newnham College, Oxford, 1947–1948. Became a Fellow of St. Anne's College, Oxford, 1948, and elected an Honorary Fellow of the same college in 1963. Married John Bayley in 1956.

Published Fiction: *Under The Net*, 1954; *Flight From The Enchanter*, 1955; *The Sandcastle*, 1957; *The Bell*, 1958; *A Severed Head*, 1961; *An Unofficial Rose*, 1962; *The Unicorn*, 1963; *The Italian Girl*, 1964; *The Red and The Green*, 1965; *The Time of The Angels*, 1966; *The Nice and the Good*, 1968; *Bruno's Dream*, 1969; *A Fairly Honourable Defeat*, 1970; *Accidental Man*, 1971.

McCARTHY, Mary, Born 1912. Educated at the Annie Wright Seminary and Vassar College. Was theatre critic for *Partisan Review*, 1937–1957. Editor of *Covici Friede*, 1937–1938. Has taught at Bard and Sarah Lawrence Colleges. Guggenheim Fellow, 1949–1950 and 1959–1960. Received the National Academy of Arts and Letters award in 1957.

Published Fiction: *The Company She Keeps*, 1942; *The Oasis*, 1949; *Cast A Cold Eye* (short stories), 1950; *The Groves of Academe*, 1952; *A Charmed Life*, 1955; *The Group*, 1963.

McCULLERS, Carson, Born 1917, Georgia. Educated at Columbus High School and at Columbia and New York Universities. Guggenheim Fellow, 1942–1943 and 1946. Received National Academy of Arts

and Letters Award in 1943 and the New York Critics' Award in 1950.
Published Fiction: *The Heart Is A Lonely Hunter*, 1940; *The Member of The Wedding*, 1946; *The Ballad Of The Sad Cafe*, 1951; *The Square Root of Wonderful*, 1958; *Clock Without Hands*, 1961; *Sweet As A Pickle and Clean As A Pig*, 1964; *Reflections in a Golden Eye*, 1967; *The Heart is a Lonely Hunter*, 1969.

NABOKOV, Vladimir, Born 1899, Russia. Educated at St. Petersburg and Cambridge University. Settled in the United States in 1940. Nabokov has taught literature and zoology (he is well-known as a lepidopterist) at various colleges and universities, including Wellesley, Harvard and Cornell.
Published Fiction in English: *Pnin*, 1957; *Bend Sinister; Invitation to a Beheading*, 1959; *Lolita*, 1959; *Nabokov's Dozen* (short stories), 1959; *Laughter in The Dark*, 1961; *Pale Fire*, 1962; *The Gift*, 1963; *The Defence*, 1964; *Despair*, 1966; *Quartet*, 1967 (four stories); *King, Queen, Knave*, 1968; *Ada*, 1969.

ORWELL, George, Born India, 1903. Educated at Eton. Served in the Indian Imperial Police. Worked in Paris and London before fighting for the Republicans in the Spanish Civil War. On his return he became a journalist and broadcaster. Orwell died in 1950.
Published Fiction: *Burmese Days*, 1934; *A Clergyman's Daughter*, 1935; *Keep The Aspidistra Flying*, 1936; *Coming Up For Air*, 1939; *Animal Farm*, 1945; *Nineteen Eighty-Four*, 1949.

PURDY, James, Born 1923, Ohio. Educated in the Midwest, the University of Chicago and the University of Madrid.
Published Fiction: *Color of Darkness*, 1957; *Malcolm*, 1959; *The Nephew*, 1960; *Children Is All*; *Cabot Wright Begins*, 1964; *Eustace Chisholm and the Works*, 1968.

ROTH, Philip, Born 1933, Newark, New Jersey. Educated at Weequahic High School and at the universities of Bucknell and Chicago. Has taught English at Chicago University, and held a Ford Foundation grant in play-writing.
Published Fiction: *Goodbye, Columbus*, 1959; *Letting Go*, 1962; *When She Was Good*, 1967; *Portnoy's Complaint*, 1969.

SALINGER, J. D., Born 1919, New York City. Educated at Manhattan public schools and the Military Academy, Paris. Served in Europe during the war with the 4th Infantry Division, United States Army. His first story was published in 1940.

Published Fiction: *The Catcher In The Rye*, 1951; *For Esmé—With Love And Squalor* (short stories), 1953; *Franny and Zooey*, 1962; *Raise High The Roofbeam, Carpenters* and *Seymour, An Introduction*, 1963.

SILLITOE, Alan, Born 1928, Nottingham. Educated at Radford Boulevard Secondary School, Nottingham. Worked in the Raleigh Bicycle Factory, Nottingham, 1942–1946. Became a wireless operator in the R.A.F. in 1946.

Published Fiction: *Saturday Night and Sunday Morning*, 1958; *The Loneliness Of The Long Distance Runner*, 1959; *The General*, 1960; *Key To The Door*, 1961; *The Ragman's Daughter* (short stories), 1963; *The Death of William Posters*, 1965; *A Tree on Fire*, 1967; *The City Adventures of Marmalade Jim*, 1967; *Guzman, Go Home!*, 1968; *Travels in Nihilon*, 1971.

SPARK, Muriel, Born Edinburgh. Educated at James Gillespie's High School for Girls, Edinburgh.

Published Fiction: *The Comforters*, 1957; *Robinson*, 1958; *The Go-Away Bird* (short stories), 1958; *Memento Mori*, 1959; *The Ballad Of Peckham Rye*, 1960; *The Bachelors*, 1960; *The Prime Of Miss Jean Brodie*, 1961; *The Girls Of Slender Means*, 1963; *The Mandelbaum Gate*, 1965; *Collected Stories*, 1967; *The Public Image*, 1968; *The Very Fine Clock*, 1969.

STOREY, David, Born 1933. Educated at the Queen Elizabeth Grammar School, Wakefield, and the Slade School of Fine Art, London. Has been a professional Rugby footballer and a television director for the B.B.C. Published Fiction: *This Sporting Life*, 1960; *Flight Into Camden*, 1961; *Radcliffe*, 1963; *In Celebration*, 1969.

STYRON, William, Born 1925, Newport Mews, Virginia. Educated at Duke University. Served in the Marine Corps.

Published Fiction: *Lie Down In Darkness*, 1951; *The Long March*, 1953; *Set This House On Fire*, 1960.

WAIN, John, Born 1925, Stoke on Trent. Educated at the High School, Newcastle-under-Lyme and St. John's College, Oxford. Lectured in English at the University of Reading, 1947–1955. Now lives from his writing.

Published Fiction: *Hurry On Down*, 1953; *Living In The Present*, 1955;

*The Contenders*, 1958; *A Travelling Woman*, 1959; *Nuncle and Other Stories*, 1960; *Strike The Father Dead*, 1962; *The Young Visitors*, 1965; *Death of the Hind Legs and Other Stories*, 1966; *The Smaller Sky*, 1967.

WATERHOUSE, Keith, Born 1929, Leeds. Educated in Leeds. Has had a career as a journalist and as a writer of scripts for films and television. Published Fiction: *There Is A Happy Land*, 1957; *Billy Liar*, 1960; *Jubb*, 1962.

WILSON, Angus, F.R.S.L., Born 1913, Bexhill. Educated at Westminster School and Merton College, Oxford. Wilson worked as an Assistant Keeper in the Department of Printed Books in the British Museum. He began to write in 1946, and in 1953 called himself 'a weekend writer only'. He is now Professor of English Literature at the University of East Anglia.

Published Fiction: *The Wrong Set* (short stories), 1949; *Such Darling Dodos* (short stories), 1951; *Hemlock and After*, 1952; *Anglo-Saxon Attitudes*, 1956; *A Bit Off the Map* (short stories), 1957; *The Middle Age of Mrs. Eliot*, 1958; *The Old Men At The Zoo*, 1961; *Late Call*, 1964; *No Laughing Matter*, 1967; *The Wrong Set and Other Stories*, 1969.

# Index